# Winter Reads

## Thor to the Rescue

## Joey Barnes 18th Book

**ISBN:** 9798744334475

# Introduction

This is the 8ᵗʰ book in my King of Obsolete Winter Road Book Series which I have written as the 18ᵗʰ book of my writing career. I have written these stories during the Covid 19 lock down in the year 2021 plus being sober too. The stories are base from 2017 to 2019 as I fulfilled my dream of winter roads and ice roads. In 1998 I became a single parent of my daughter Xena who grew up around the winter roads and ice roads. Our way of life at the end of the world of having fun making a living is enjoyed around the world through my website since 2004.

**www.kingofobsolete.ca**

thansk

# INDEX

## Winter Road Introduction

This introduction is for the 8 books of my Winter Road Book Series. Since my readers are worldwide as my Kingdom Followers, I will use the introduction to explain what winter roads are and how they came about. Canadian Winter Roads are very different from the Ice Roads made famous by the TV show called Ice Road Truckers which gave me my 15 seconds of fame. People have to remember that the TV show Ice Road Truckers was a form of entertainment like the Playboy Channel. Plus, the TV networks spent a lot of time and money to make the show a success around the world. I tip my hat to the TV network because I am still enjoying my 15 seconds of fame from all the marketing they have done. I will include a story on the filming we did but it will be more on the film crew and how they did their jobs in the cold Canadian winter. All other information or stories I will let the TV network tell those stories because they paid a lot of money to film and make the show.

A Canadian Winter Road is a road built through the boreal forest in northern Manitoba where I live. The boreal forest are small trees growing that never get big in diameter because the sandy soil and cold weather we live in. The boreal forest is known for the muskeg which can be bottomless, but the permafrost will keep a tracked machine from sinking too far down before the machine can be recovered. The winter roads where I live on the west side of the province of Manitoba are totally different then the winter roads on the east side of the province. There is a huge different between the road system because the east side winter roads are smooth and flat. These roads started off as Cat Train trails where one caterpillar dozer machine would pull 4-6 loaded winter freighting sleighs to deliver freight. The easiest way for a Cat Train to travel was across the frozen lake because the frozen lake was smooth and flat. But in the mid-1960s the company Sigfusson which wrote the book called the Sigfussons Roads started to move the Cat Trains off the frozen lakes and into the boreal forests for safety. The reason why they moved off the lakes and into the boreal forest was because too many Cat Trains were falling through the ice. Cat Trains have been around since the 1930s and traveled mostly on the frozen lakes because it was easier. But the over the years the Cat Trains got bigger and bigger hauling heavier loads. The heavier loads found the bad ice on the frozen lakes more and more. Sigfusson started moving the Cat Trains trails off the bad lakes and by the mid-1970s most to the Cat Train trails were off the frozen lakes they could bypass. There were still lots of Cat Train trails being used across the frozen lakes.

As the communities on the east side of Manitoba got bigger and bigger with more people living in the communities. The slow-moving Cat Trains were being replaced by the semi-trucks of the 1970s. The semi-trucks traveled faster on the Cat Trails that were being dragged to make them smooth for the trucks to travel on. With the semi-trucks hauling from the highway across the roads built in the boreal forest to the remote communities. This saved on double handling the freight from highway trucks to the winter freighting sleighs. The days were numbered for the Cat Trains as they were becoming obsolete. The last known Cat Trains of the official era of the Cat Trains last hauled in 1986 as a bunch of worn-out equipment and men because everything got older including the men. It took a special breed of men to run the Cat Trains because fear of falling through the ice on the frozen lake was there every minute of the day. Now the Manitoba Government took over the winter road system in Manitoba and improved the system which was surprising for a government to do. The roads became smoother and well maintained with lots of local people of communities were employed.

But the west side of the winter roads were a lot different, and nothing really changed. All winter roads remained as ice roads because on the west side the boreal forest was rock and more rocks plus muskeg. The Cat Trains never went through the boreal forest unless crossing from frozen lake to frozen lake. Then when the semi-trucks took over from the Cat Trains, the winter roads stayed on the frozen lakes as ice roads until 1997. That was the year when there was not enough ice to make the ice roads to the 3-remote communities accessed from Lynn Lake Manitoba. The Manitoba Government started a big push to make winter roads through the boreal forest to these remote communities. This involved 330kms of new road to Tadoule Lake MB as the main winter road. Then the road branched off for 125kms to Lac Brochet MB. Also, the winter road branched off for 60kms to Brochet MB too. This winter road was built over rocks and more rocks, then across muskeg and long beside huge eskers of sand left by the glaciers from the ice age. This was unforgiven rough terrain which took a long time for the government to make a decent winter road for traveling.

I will start my 1st book in the series; Winter Roads: My Struggles from 1996 through to 2007. Then continue with my 2nd book in the series; Winter Roads: Head Hanger from 2008 through to 2009. My 3rd book in the series; Winter Roads: White Suburban from 2010 through to 2011. My 4th book in the series; Winter Roads: Dream Team the year 2012. My 5th book in the series; Winter Roads: 15 Seconds of Fame the year 2013. My 6th book in the series; Winter Roads: Russian Roulette the year 2014. My 7th book in the series; Winter Roads: Never Give Up from 2015 through to 2016. My 8th book in the series; Winter Roads: Thor to the Rescue from 2017 through to 2019. These books will be on my experiences with winter and ice roads which will include my 15 seconds of fame on the Ice Road Truckers show.

## Chapter 1
**Big Storm**


After returning from the mining convention in the South which was 1200km from Winnipeg MB in November 2016. Xena and I started getting ready for building winter drill roads which are the same as winter roads but narrower. The government winter roads that allow access to the remote communities are built 4-Caterpillar dozer blades wide. The winter drill roads we built were only 1-Caterpillar dozer blade wide. The winter drill roads had to be a road of least restrictions this meaning using trails or open areas wherever possible. The government permits even stated we could not bulldoze trees down if we could go around them. With the help of Zoom Earth and lots of ski-dooing and snowshoeing to find the easy way to access the drill area that the Australian exploration company wanted to drill. The Australians we called them the OZies because working on the mineral claims that I had optioned to them had to be done in secret. Now that I had optioned my mineral claims to people who lived in a hot climate. That only seen Canada through the TV show Ice Road Truckers was not the best thing I could have done. These OZies had a hard time understanding that the muskeg ground had to be worked as the snows came that covered the ground to insulate it. Once the snow got deep in covering the ground it would not freeze because the snow now insulated the ground. The Ozies thought that Canada just froze over, and the drill equipment could drive out on the frozen ground to begin drilling. Plus, the OZies had money for the project raised on the Australian Stock Market which meant it cannot be wasted or spent before the project officially begins. I had to use Facebook posts and pictures from the people of the remote communities that were trying to get an early start on building winter roads for their communities. The non-stop rain we got in the rainy season for the Great White North started in September and never stopped until the snow came in October. The muskegs, lakes and creek were all high water then the snows came, and it never stopped snowing. I sent the OZies weekly updates on the conditions that WHO-ville was under with the worse winter freeze up that I had ever seen in the 21-years I had been living in the Kingdom. But the OZies did not see a problem because the drilling equipment was booked for January 10, 2017, start up with a drill program of 10-holes that need 30kms of winter drill roads built plus drill pads. "Yes", the drill rig can sit on almost frozen muskeg to drill a hole down looking for nickel ore. But what happens when they try to pull the heavy drill rods out of the hole. The drill rig will sink very quicky trying to lift all the weight of the drill rods. The drill pads had to be solid frozen ground as if they are made of 3-feet of cement. This was no problem because we used the Linn Tractor to haul water to flood the drill pads when we had built the winter drill roads.

(Linn Tractor hauling water from the frozen lake)

But to get these winter drill roads we just went ahead and built them with ski-dooing to pack the snow to get the muskeg to freeze. We did not really care what the OZies thought or did because this was what we had to do for them to be able to drill for nickel mineral on January 10, 2017. We had kept in touch with the contractors working on building the government winter roads because they were having a hard time. The Brochet road crew always had the winter road to the community plowed out as a road long before the government arrived on January 09 each year to open it officially. Not this year, the Brochet road crew was struggling to get even a rough road plowed opened. There was way too much snow on top of the non-frozen muskeg plus any low areas were full of water under the snow. The road crew had to plow and then wait for it to freeze then plow some more. They were basically building a winter road twice and the government was not offering any extra money or bonus to get the winter road open. It was not until the end of January when the winter road to Brochet MB was opened, and the fuel semi-trucks headed in over a rough road. I had parted way with the fuel company after 12 years because of the Dumbass manager. When the broken semi-trucks came off the winter road broken, I just smiled, they had to limp to Thompson MB to wait in the long lines for repairs. I told the truck drivers that the fuel company had a good thing going with me doing the repairs plus all the free stuff that I had given them. The truck drivers were not happy but when they stop by the Kingdom to see if I would fix something quickly, I did point out that the fuel company had an outstanding invoice that was not paid. Of course, the truck drivers would pass the information on to head office to have the outstanding invoice paid but that never happened. Also, when the truck drivers came to the Kingdom, they could not believe how busy the place was. The Kingdom was now the hub of the OZies drill program with a helicopter and 29-people running around making the drill program a success. I was now working smarter not harder for the first time in my life. But for my good customers and friends, I would take time out to fix or help them out because their money put food on my table during the tough times.

With the drill program started successfully because I did not listen to the OZies telling me how to do business in the Great White North. The helicopter was being used to move the drill rig around one piece at a time. That was the only way it could be done with not all of the muskeg ground being really frozen except for our winter drill roads we had made. My ex-fiancé the cop was back and forth from Grief Rapids to WHO-ville as she was fighting crime in both places being the lead cop. One of the problems the cops were having was finding new cops to move to the Great White North to live in the cop houses for the next 3-years. Most of the new cops' families wanted nothing to do with living at the end of the world. Plus, it was harder and harder for the cops to live with the criminals in town. The cops had their own fancy airplanes to fly the cops around to work the shifts where staffing was short. But if the weather was bad and the cop plane could not land then the cops from WHO-ville and Grief Rapids covered both communities. My ex-fiancé would stop by the Kingdom when she was in WHO-ville to see what I was doing or for some cuddling on the couch. My ex-fiancé was impressed the day she stopped by the Kingdom to see the helicopter flying in and out of the Kingdom while we enjoyed a coffee to chat about the good times of being engaged. She also could not get over the number of people working in the Kingdom in the buildings I had set up for playing with the drill core. Now my ex-fiancé was not saying a word when I teased her about "dumping" me because I did not have a "real job" back in 2010. I had bettered myself with being on national TV around the world which my ex-fiancé got to watch on "my" TV she took with "my" white suburban. But my ex-fiancé did the like the helicopter in and out of the Kingdom and asked lots of questions about it which I really knew nothing about. The only thing I knew about helicopters was there was the graduating class pictures when helicopter pilots graduate. But never a class reunion pictures because on paper a helicopter cannot fly like a bubble bee. After enjoying a coffee with my ex-fiancé, she had to go back to work making new friends in WHO-ville and left the Kingdom with promises of her stopping by later to do bad things to me. Of course, I knew it was all lies, because anytime she made plans to do bad things to me, she had to do cop things that came up at the last minute.

The weather network on the computer was forecasting a big snowstorm coming from Alberta which we thought was wrong. The big snowstorm would dump all the snow in Alberta then when it arrived in WHO-ville it would be not that great or big. As the saying goes, "the storm would have fizzled out". The helicopter pilot was watching the weather forecast too because the weather effects the flying of the helicopter. I assured the helicopter pilot that the big snowstorm would not be that big because they never are. I grew up in the South and had seen bad snowstorms that closed everything down for 2-days of more. Now I had been in the Great White North since my DIEvorce 23-years ago. I had never seen a snowstorm bad enough to close everything down for 2-day like what they got in the South. I was so wrong because my friends on Facebook in Alberta were posting the events of the bad snowstorm as it passed by them. In theory the snowstorm should had "fizzled" out by the time it arrived in WHO-ville. The first day the snowstorm hit was not bad, and we could still drive around and go back and forth to the drill rig on the mineral claims. But the second day the Gods were angry, and we got the big snowstorm like I had growing up in the South. The wind was unreal and never stopped with more and more snow coming. I had to plow the Kingdom several times to keep access for the people working the drill program in and out of the yard. The third day of the snowstorm was still bad, and all roads were officially closed for the first time in my life living up here. None of the drill program people left the motel where everyone was staying. Plus, Xena and I just ski-dooed over to the motel to touch base with everyone there. The nightshift crew on the drill rig had used the satellite phone to call the motel to say they could not even ski-doo out to the highway to get back to WHO-ville. The most important thing for the drill crew at the drill rig was the water line that was pumping water 2kms to the drill rig. When drilling in the bedrock, the drill rig using lots of water to keep the drill hole clean and cool while drilling. With 2kms of 1" rubber water line laying in the snow to keep from freezing. The main concern for the drill crew was to keep the pump at the lake running. Plus, everything at the drill rig was based on 12-hours shifts which everything was then fueled up. The drill crew at the drill rig had stopped drilling when the snowstorm got bad at 2am and fueled everything up to wait out the snowstorm. Now the 12-hours were coming up for the pump at the lake to run out of fuel then stop pumping water the 2kms to the drill rig. As long as the water in the 1" rubber hose was moving it was not freezing.

Xena and I chatted with everyone at the motel, and no one were interested in coming with me on the ski-doos to help the drillers at the drill rig. There was 19 people who were all males and people who lift weights to stay in shape. None of these people offered to help so it was Xena and me ski-dooing 10kms to the drill rig because all the roads were blocked with snow. Xena just laughed at the fact no one had offered to take her place in ski-dooing but she had done the job of a man all her life. It was hard ski-dooing in the deep snow on the road to the drill rig because the highway was blowing in with solid snow. Plus, we were snow blind with the blowing snow and could not see anything when the road came to an open spot in the trees. We both knew if we could make the winter drill road, then we would be in the trees, it would get better. We were so glad to arrive on our winter drill roads and drive the ski-doos to the drill rig which only had about 8" of fresh snow. The drill crew were happy to see us because we had brought them food supplies from the motel. They had only taken enough food for the 12-hour work shift not 24-hours that that had almost been at the drill. Next Xena and I ski-dooed down to the lake where we had left the Linn Tractor. Only made sense to leave the Linn Tractor down by the lake because we had been using the machine to haul water to freeze the drill pads to make them frozen solid. The Linn Tractor fired right up and now I drove the Linn Tractor back to the drill to get the fuel needed for the pump. The winter drill roads in the open areas had drifted in to be almost 5-feet of snow but the Linn Tractor had no problems. The Linn Tractor was built in 1945 to be the highway truck for the Cat Train Trails with skis on the front instead of wheels. It took us about an hour to get the fuel to the pump by the lake and that keep the pump running to save the water line from freezing.

(Linn Tractor busting through the snow drifts)

The snowstorm never stopped but Xena and I kept going because we had no choice. I grew up to these big snowstorms in the South, but this was Xena first big snowstorm at the age of 19-years old. When the drillers were happy and everything running smoothly for them to just watch over the drill rig but not be drilling. Xena and I headed back to WHO-ville with me driving the Linn Tractor towing the ski-doo I had driven to the drill site.

(Xena and I driving down the highway)

The Linn Tractor was made for driving down a closed road with lots of snow on it because it was a highway truck for the Cat Train Trails. As we drove through the streets of WHO-ville there was lots of vehicles stuck and abandon on the snow blocked streets. Xena and I did not have time to help the vehicles stuck besides there was no one around because they were abandoned. Back in the

Kingdom, the Linn Tractor had to be fueled up and serviced to go back out for 7pm crew change at the drill. The drillers had been there over 24-hours so they will be glad to get back to the motel. Xena did not have to come for the crew change because I figured the Linn Tractor would have no problems. When I picked up the drillers at 6pm for the crew change at the motel. That would leave us lots of time to travel the 10kms to the drill site. The whole safety and success of not freezing the water line was based on old obsolete equipment that I owned as being the King of Obsolete. The new fancy ski-doos did not like the deep snow same as the vehicles with 4x4 could not make it around in the deep snow. The fancy new helicopter sitting at the airport for 3-days now only to fly when the weather conditions were prefect. The Linn Tractor did excellent driving through WHO-ville then out on the road to the drill site. When we arrived at the drill site, the drillers that had been there so long were happy to see the lights of the Linn Tractor coming towards the drill rig in the darkness plus almost white out conditions. The drillers chatted with each other briefly then I drove back to WHO-ville with the driller crew. They had been at the drill site and only see how bad the snowstorm was in the trees and down by the lake. Now they got to see how bad the storm really was when we arrived in WHO-ville. The Linn Tractor made it so easy to drive along so the drill crew could see all the vehicle stuck and everything closed. The drill crew was so happy to arrive back at the motel because they were hungry and needed a shower to warm up. I then headed back to the Kingdom and parked the Linn Tractor in case I was called out again for a rescue mission.

I was on standby call, but I needed my pain medication Vodka to relax my sore body from driving the Linn Tractor and ski-dooing too. As my Vodka started taste really good, my telephone rang, and it was my ex-fiancé calling. When I answered the telephone excepting her to tell me that she was wearing a sexy outfit and would email me pictures now that she knew I was home. But instead, she told me she was still in her cop uniform and wearing her gun belt. Once she said that I had no naughty thoughts of her crossing my mind for some reason. Now my ex-fiancé was total professional and acting like the lead cop because she needed answers and ideas now. The so-called road to Thompson MB had been closed for 3-days now with the big snowstorm drifted the so-called road in to make it impassable everywhere. The helicopters based in Thompson MB hoped to be flying late the next day but had to fly elsewhere. My ex-fiancé now wanted all information on the helicopter flying in and out of the Kingdom because she will need it for official cop business. I told my ex-fiancé to have the cops here go to the motel and chat with the pilot and the Canadian people in charge of the OZie drill program. She hung up the telephone without saying goodbye or promising to do bad things to me later. Oh well, I was used to her hanging up the telephone which I had to drink my pain medication Vodka. In the morning the snowstorm was still as strong as it was for the last 3-days, but it was to stop and clear up in late afternoon. Xena and I ski-dooed to the motel to check out what was happening with the drill program. The drillers had good luck in keeping the water line and pump going at the drill. If the water line had frozen then it would be close to 3-days to thaw out the frozen line to be able to drill again. Everyone was talking about how the cops had arrived and took control of the helicopter once it could begin flying safely when the snowstorm ended. Nobody could figure out how the cops knew who to talk to plus knew all the details of the helicopter. I never told anyone in the drill program that the lead cop in Grief Rapids was my ex-fiancé plus no one would believe me anyways. With no helicopter to support the drill program because the cops "official" took charge of the machine. The whole drill program was now based on my old obsolete equipment plowing the winter drill roads and moving the drill to the next drill location.

The government department of highways had way too much work to do to worry about the 7-miles of highway to where the winter drill roads started on the mineral claims. Xena and I will just plow everything to open it up for the drill crews and the other crews to be able to work on the mineral claims. We were able to start plowing around 6pm at night when the wind and the snowstorm started to die down. It was at midnight when Xena and I arrived with the 2-small cats to the drill rig where the driller crew were waiting for us. Our support vehicle that followed us as we plowed was the drill crew for the crew change. We had plowed all the roads for a vehicle to follow and have access to the drill rig. Once Xena and I had plowed out the drill rig then we had to plow the road to the lake so the pump could be fueled up. When the drill crew was happy, we plowed the other roads of the mineral claims.

It was 10am in the morning when we had returned the Kingdom with the small cats plowing all the way. The big snowstorm had ended around 1am and by 3am the night skies were clear, and we could watch the Northern Lights dance in the clear skies. Watching and enjoying the Northern Lights made it all worthwhile working all night. Back in the Kingdom, Xena ski-dooed to her house in WHO-ville to sleep then I needed my pain medication Vodka to help me sleep. I was about to fall asleep when the telephone rang which was my ex-fiancé. Now I had been enjoying my pain medication Vodka which made it hard for me to talk on the telephone to my ex-fiancé in a business manner. She was wearing her uniform and had her gun belt on. Even when I asked what colour of undies she was wearing under her cop uniform she would not answer but change the subject. Being colour blind she could have told me any colour in the rainbow because her undies would look to be different shades of grey to me. My ex-fiancé asked me questions which I now answered correctly and seriously because I had realized that this was an official business call by her as the lead cop. When my ex-fiancé had her questions answered with the information, I had given her. She just hung up the telephone without saying goodbye or answering me on what colour her undies were. Oh well, this was normal and maybe she was going to stop by the Kingdom later for me to personally find out the colour. I then went into a deep sleep until the helicopter landed in the Kingdom which I thought was strange. All the roads in and out of WHO-ville were closed and the helicopter was to be flying for the cops under the emergency act.

The pilot was now standing at the door to my house and was asking for oil which I thought was strange. I was not awake and still officially drunk from my pain medication Vodka. The pilot then explained that the semi-trucks up the winter roads that are stranded needed oil for the motors. Ok, now that made sense because the semi-trucks had been running for close to 4-days and the motors leak and use oil when not running at high rpms. The cop that was with the pilot flying around checking on the semi-trucks told me the fuel tanker semi-trucks had grouped in with other semi-trucks that were not fuel tankers. The fuel tanker semi-trucks were sharing the fuel out of the fuel tankers to keep the other semi-trucks running. But the motor oil was in need because the truck drivers had used up any extra oil, they had in the semi-truck storage boxes. The cop and pilot figured there was 24-vehicles stranded up on the winter roads that start off the Kinoosoa Rally Road. As I get the oil that I had in stock in my oil shed for the helicopter to fly up to the stranded semi-trucks. The cop and pilot figure they would be flying back and forth for the next 4-days checking on the stranded semi-trucks. The road crews on the winter roads had to dig out their equipment that was left on the winter road when the snowstorm hit. Then they could start plowing the winter roads open. The winter roads had drifted right in because they are narrow roads to start with. The helicopter pilot was happy to be flying these long trips all over the winter road system because he had spent 6-weeks only flying the drill rig around. Now it was fun flying and seeing the Great White North too. The cop that was along to document the people in the stranded vehicles and make the disscisions on what to do, wanted to be a helicopter pilot himself but could not afford the training. As the helicopter took off from the Kingdom, I went back to bed to sleep after a good shot of Vodka to close my eyes.

I was early in the evening when my ex-fiancé was calling me still wearing her cop uniform and gun belt. She had more and more questions which I just answered then decided to stay awake because I knew if I went back to sleep, I would wake up later and then could not go back to sleep. I had a hard time staying awake because my body only wanted to sleep because we had worked almost 48-hours straight through. When I check the news on my computer since I do not have TV. Who-ville made the national news for the big snowstorm. Plus, all the road around WHO-ville which officially closed for the last 4-days. The news people were saying another 2-days until the road could be open to the South. For the first time in my life, I had witnessed the roads around WHO-ville closed with no access to the South. This might be big drama for some people, but I had enough pain medication and supplies to last a long time. The daily mail service from the South will only be bring me bills not money. The beer vendor will run out of beer because the beer truck from the South only comes on Wednesday. Since I drink professionally, the people of WHO-ville who run out of booze beverages will want to be my new best friend who will not be happening. I was able to stay awake until midnight then I let my pain medication Vodka closed my eyes until the morning.

I was woken up by the telephone ringing which I answered. It was my ex-fiancé saying she was still wearing her cop uniform and gun belt with more question she needed answers for. Once she had my answers, my ex-fiancé then hung up the telephone without saying goodbye which I knew she was going to do. After I had my morning coffee and updated my website for my Kingdom Followers around the world to enjoy. I then got ready to see what was happening with the drill program. I met Xena at the motel where all the people for the drill program was staying. The Canadian people in charge are trying to figure out how the cops know so much about the helicopter and what was happening up the winter roads with the stranded semi-trucks. The cops had come early this morning to have the helicopter fly 2-cops up to a stranded semi-truck, but no reasons given. I just listen to everyone talk about what was going on and did not say anything. The cops had figured the winter roads would re-open soon, but they still might need the helicopter until all strand semi-trucks were off the winter roads. This was still a state of emergency with people lives at risk up on the winter roads. After Xena and I were done and had touched base with the drill program, we returned back to the Kingdom. We had lots to do, and we always seemed to be behind because we do good quality work. It was later in the day when the helicopter had returned with only the pilot no cops. The pilot when on to tell us that he had flown the cops up to one of the stranded semi-trucks that was a short distance from a big group. The helicopter pilot and the cop had check on each stranded semi-truck after the snowstorm had ended. But this one truck driver was acting different and different each visit. The truck driver had a satellite phone and during the night he was making lots of calls to the cop shop because he finally "snapped". Then at the break of day light, the helicopter pilot and 2-cops flew up to the fellow who "snapped", and it was not a good scene. It took all 3 of the guys to wrestle and get the truck driver that "snapped" into the helicopter and back to WHO-ville. The helicopter was landed at the hospital for the doctor to give the truck driver who snapped a shot that made him relax. The helicopter pilot said his greatest fear was the truck driver trying to jump out of the helicopter while flying and in handcuffs. The only thing I told the helicopter pilot it was a good thing I had staked these mineral claims and optioned them to the OZies. If not, then there would have been no drill program with a helicopter stationed at the airport when the big snowstorm came. The helicopter came in very handy for the stranded truck drivers. The helicopter pilot thanked me and said he enjoyed all the flying he had done with the cops after the big snowstorm.

When the day was finally done, I was relaxing in the house when a cop car pulled in my driveway and parked beside the house. Whoever was driving the cop car knew not to block in the buildings for the drill crew because they are in and out of the Kingdom all night. When I answered the door to the house, it was my ex-fiancé wearing a long black coat not the cop winter coat. As soon as I opened the door, she walked right in and did not wait for me to invite her into my house. She then said she was off duty from being the cop after working non-stop through the big snowstorm like what Xena and I had done. I then asked if she needed some of my pain medication Vodka to take the pain away which she replied "Yes". She also asked for me to mix her a good drink with only a little bit of Cherry Kool-Aid for colouring. I had no problem in mixing my ex-fiancé a good drink to take the pain away. When the drink was made, I passed her the drink which she drank in one shot then asked for another one. Oh my, was all I had to say as I mixed her another which she drank very fast too. I then reminded her that I am a professional drinker, and she was drinking way too fast and was officially unable to drive or leave the Kingdom. My ex-fiancé then looked at me as she stood in my kitchen with a smile on her face. I am not sure how she did it, but the long black coat was now unbuttoned and on the floor of my kitchen. I was all smiles because she was standing in front of me only wear lingerie which she did not buy at Walmart. I then ask the colour of the sexy outfit she was wearing because I am colour blind. Her only reply back was the colour "orange" as she walked past me and into my bedroom. Being colour blind I had to think to myself if the colour of "orange" was sexy in the eyes a non-colour blind person. As I am thinking, I brushed my teeth and freshen up in the bathroom while my ex-fiancé was in my bedroom. I think I took too long in the bathroom because when I crawled into my bed, my ex-fiancé was sound asleep. The pain medication Vodka in good stiff drinks plus working non-stop during the big snowstorm for days had burnt her out with exhaustion. Now she was in a deep sleep because that was what she needed. In the morning she was still sleeping when I got and had breakfast then off to the drill site to plow the winter drill roads. Everyone on the drill program had seen the cop car parked in my driveway that never moved all night and all day. The helicopter pilot was the one who figured out how the cops knew what to do with the helicopter. I was telling my ex-fiancé how she should handle the problems with stranded semi-trucks up the winter roads. The helicopter pilot was in shock when I told him that the lead cop was my ex-fiancé. He told me he would have never believed it in a million years that I was engaged to the cop. I just smiled and was glad she had listened to what I had suggested for her to do with the stranded semi-trucks up the winter roads. When I returned to the Kingdom near 7pm with the plowing done on the drill site. My ex-fiancé was gone back to Grief Rapids and left me a note on the table saying "I" missed out on enjoying the "orange" outfit. When I had read that note I just smiled because she was the one that fell asleep after working non-stop in a state of emergency.

## Chapter 2
**Kinoosao Snow**


It was only 4-days later the weather forecast was for more snow and we were still digging out from the big snowstorm. I knew there was no way my small cats could plow the huge snowbanks on all the winter drill roads. Xena and I decided to go to Kinoosao Sk and pick the big cats that we used for loading the barge that traveled to Brochet MB on Reindeer Lake. We had stopped any dealings with the barge in 2016 because of un-paid invoices that we knew would never get paid. I had wanted to bring the 2-big cats back to the Kingdom and now was the perfect time to do it. The government highways department had the local contractor with new style dozers plow open the Kinoosao Rally Road because it had drifted in with the big snowstorm. I knew anything to do with the government it would be ½-job and I was correct. Xena and I left late in the afternoon to travel to Kinoosao SK because that was when the heavy snowfall warning was issued for northern Manitoba again. This was not a planned trip, and we just left the Kingdom on moment's notice. But I did send a Facebook message to Kinoosao to say we were coming. Not sure why because they never reply to any of my messages in the past. The Screaming Ford was always chained up and I knew this little quick trip was going to be a fun trip where a film crew would get good filming. But in the past when I had asked Hollywood to send a film crew to join us their usual reply was the same each time "too dangerous". The Kinoosao Rally Road was perfect until the start of the winter roads with the road well plowed. But 10-feet passed the start of the winter roads, the Kinoosao Rally Road now turned in to a plowed cat trail. "Yes", the big snowstorm had dumped enough snow that the Kinoosao Rally Road had to be plowed out using the local contractor's new style Caterpillar dozers. This would not have been a problem, but the government was cheap and did not want to pay for a quality job. The operators on the Caterpillar dozers were airplane pilots that fly the float airplanes from the water base in the summer months to the American Fishing Lodges. Pilots are taught to watch the gauges on the airplane and the new style Caterpillar dozers had gauges too that even told the operator of the speed they were traveling. The pilots just watched the speedometers when operating the Caterpillar dozers to plow the 50kms to Kinoosao to open the roads as fast as they could. But when the pilots came to any hill to maintain speed like flying an airplane, they lifted the blade on the Caterpillar dozers. Less snow base on the Kinoosao Rally Road to plow off the road when climbing the hill. As long as the speedometer on the new style cat dozer was showing the same speed going up the hill or down the hill everyone was happy except for me.

(Screaming Ford at the start of the winter roads)

The Screaming Ford all chained up on the rear drive wheels did not like climbing the hills that had an 8" snow base still left on the base of the road. The rear-ends on the Screaming Ford would then bunny hop trying to dig for traction. Now if the pilots had plowed the road like I had done for the 2-years when I had a "real job". I did not care about the flat parts of the Kinoosao Rally Road but worried about the hills. All the hills were cut right down for traction when I operated the obsolete Champion grader for Buddy Barry. The Kinoosao Rally Road was like the winter roads, if the vehicle cannot climb a hill or cross an ice field then the whole length of the road should be closed.

(the cat trail they called a plowed road)

Once I figured out how the pilots plowed the Kinoosao Rally Road then I had to drive the Screaming Ford according to the conditions. That meant drive the 8V71 detroit even harder to climb the snow packed hills with making it scream for mercy. The little quick trip to Kinoosao should have only taken 2-hours to travel the 100kms. But we did in 4-hours and never got stuck with the Screaming Ford. There were several times I just about stuck with the Screaming Ford because of the way the pilots plowed the roads watching the speedometer. Oh well, a film crew would have had a good time with us. When we arrived in Kinoosao, the pilots never plowed an inch of snow that they did not have to plow or get paid to plow. We had to leave the Screaming Ford in the middle of the narrow road that could only fit 1-vehicle. The pink crew cab had the gas-powered welder in the back, and we let it run to plug in the blocked heater on the D6 Caterpillar that I had left in Kinoosao. As the block heater warmed up the D6 Caterpillar, Xena and I ate our supper in the pink crew cab. It was now dark, and I figured the D6 Caterpillar needed at least 2-hours of heating to be able to start. The D6 Caterpillar had not run since last fall which was 5-months ago, but the motor was always a good starter. As we ate, there were lights came up from behind us and it was the locals coming back to Kinoosao. They had heard we had headed to Kinoosao and knew we would make it over the terribly plowed road. They were correct that we had made it and broke a trail for them to follow. But now they could not understand why the Screaming Ford was blocking the last part of the road for them to get home. These people were not thinking clearly being storm stayed for almost 10-day. Then not being able to drive the last 400-feet to be stuck in front of their house. I explained to the locals that I had to get the D6 Caterpillar running to be able to plow out the last part of the road to Kinoosao. Then I can move the Screaming Ford. But the locals just did not understand and were getting upset that they were so close to home but cannot get home. I then point up that if it was not for Xena and I coming over the Kinoosao Rally Road they would most likely be stuck on the road in a bad spots where the pilots had lifted the blade of the dozers to maintain speed.

As more vehicles showed up and parked behind the Screaming Ford, I gave up trying to explain to the locals. They should not be mad at me for blocking the road. They should be mad at the government for only paying for ½-job on plowing the Kinoosao Rally Road. I told Xena will have to ether the D6 Caterpillar to make the motor start if it liked it or not. The D6 Caterpillar was under water for 3-years before we got it in 2003. We did nothing to the motor except drain the water, mud and the fish out of it. Plus, it was not going to be the first time the motor had been ether started because the D6 Caterpillar was needed now. The D6 Caterpillar fired right up with the ether start and I had a coffee while the motor warmed up. After coffee, I plowed a big area behind the Screaming Ford for the locals to park their vehicles out of the way so I could plow an area to turn the Screaming Ford around. When I went to move the Screaming Ford, we made sure to tell the locals to wait until the Screaming Ford was parked. Then I would plow the last 400-feet to Kinoosao for the locals to drive to their homes. Of course, no one listened and as soon as there was just enough space as I backed up the Screaming Ford, one vehicle drove passed the Screaming Ford only to get stuck in the deep snow. Now I had to get on the D6 Caterpillar and pull the stuck vehicle out because it was blocking the Screaming Ford from completing the turn around. When we pulled the stuck vehicle out of the deep snow, Xena and I both told the driver to stay put and not move. But as soon as the tow chain was unhooked the driver sped off thinking that driving fast in too the deep snow on the road would keep the vehicle from getting stuck. The vehicle only went a few feet farther then where it was stuck before. Both Xena and I were getting "pissed" at these people not listening because we are not getting paid for any of this. This whole trip to Kinoosao and all this extra plowing was costing me money, and no one will repay me for my time or effort. Now that I was mad, I hopped on the D6 Caterpillar and plowed the rest of the way to Kinoosao leaving the stuck vehicle where it was. I could not back up because the other vehicles waiting were right behind the D6 Caterpillar. Once I had the road plowed then we pulled out the stuck vehicle and off it went to Kinoosao. Nobody stopped and thanked Xena or I for helping them out which they would have never made it over the Kinoosao Rally Road if we had not broken trail.

Now we loaded up the second big cat that was parked beside the D6 Caterpillar. We used the 30,000lbs Wicked Winch to drag the non-running cat up on to the beavertail trailer. We are not wasting any more time than we had wasted already. With the big cat loaded and chained down on the beavertail trailer. I then drove the D6 Caterpillar plowing the Kinoosao Rally Road to the top of the big hill just outside of town. Xena gave me a ride back to the Screaming Ford in the pink crew cab and even she said the big hill had way too much snowpack on it for the pink crew cab to climb up in 4x4. I had spent about an hour cutting the snowpack off the big hill because the pilots had made a mess when plowing in the new style dozers. The Screaming Ford climbed the big hill no problem with the tire chains on the tires getting enough traction. At the top of the big hill, we loaded the D6 Caterpillar on the beavertail trailer which was big mistake. I should have plowed the Kinoosoa Rally Road for another 1km to cut the thick snowpack off the road left behind by the pilots in the new style dozers. The Screaming Ford came around a little sloped corner climbing the little hill. But the thick snow packed made the Screaming Ford start to bunny hop as the back wheels tried to dig for traction. When I spun out on the little hill, I should have unloaded the D6 Caterpillar and pushed the Screaming Ford up the little hill. The beavertail trailer was at a bad lean which would have made the D6 Caterpillar only fall off the side of the trailer. I decided to back up the Screaming Ford to make the beavertail trailer level to be safe. Wrong, the beavertail trailer now slid sideways into the ditch and against the toothpick trees. My night had gone from bad to worse very quickly. They say history repeats itself which it had just done. In 2009 I had the same thing happened as what I was now dealing with, but I was smarter. I know that the D6 Caterpillar will fall sideways off the beavertail trailer but now the toothpick trees will assist in stopping me from sliding. When the D6 Caterpillar was off the side of the trailer. The track had fallen off and the cat broke through the crust of the muskeg water in the ditch.

Xena and I could not give up and we worked for 4-hours at -30c to get the track back on then get the Screaming Ford up the little hill. We had just gotten the everything up on the only straight part of the road to enjoy a warmup and coffee. A friend of mine from Kinoosao had ski-dooed back to Kinoosao late last night from Brochet MB on the frozen Reindeer Lake. Now he and his daughter were driving her small car and trying to make it to WHO-ville for a doctor's appointment. But the little car was getting stuck on the Kinoosao Rally Road where we had not plowed. I told my friend that the Screaming Ford cannot propel itself on the Kinoosao Rally Road where the pilots plowing with the new style dozers had lifted the blade to maintain speed. It was a group decision that we had to help each other out with plowing the Kinoosao Rally Road with the D6 Caterpillar. My friend could drive the Screaming Ford because he grew up driving semi-trucks back in the day like me. His daughter will follow behind the Screaming Ford in her little car. Xena and I would take turns driving the D6 Caterpillar that way we had time to warm up in the pink crew cab in the lead.

(Screaming Ford with the 2 big cats on the trailer)

We did this for 25kms back over the Kinoosao Rally Road which we made sure to plow all hills and curves right down. When the Kinoosao Rally Road got better because the government highways grader had plowed a little bit of the road. Then we loaded up the D6 Caterpillar on the back of the beavertail trailer. My friend was late for his doctor's appointment in WHO-ville but he was not stuck on the road in a the deep snow base.

It felt good to be back driving the Screaming Ford at a great speed of 25mph compared to the D6 Caterpillar plowing in 5th gear at 5mph. The Screaming Ford with the 2-big cats on the beavertail trailer enjoyed the Kinoosao Rally Road with making the 8V71 detroit scream for mercy. It was nice to arrive back in the Kingdom after leaving 27-hours before and having no sleep. My pain medication Vodka was calling my name which closed my eyes very quickly. When I woke up at 3am for my "pee" the snowstorm had hit WHO-ville with lots of snow coming down. I knew in the morning I would be plowing the winter drill roads with the D6 Caterpillar because the small cats had done all they could do.

## Chapter 3
## KoO TV Show

The snows never stopped for the rest of the winter which made it harder and harder to plow snow. I had never seen this much snow in the Great White North that never seem to stop. The drill program ran in to the month of June 2017 which meant I had to leave the D6 Caterpillar out at the mineral claims South of WHO-ville. The smaller cats were loaded on the trailer to take out to the mineral claims when needed then brought back to the Kingdom. Each time a small cat was needed, it had a different job to do. In the Kingdom we had 16-cats to choose from to make the job easier plus they were all obsolete cats too. The winter road semi-trucks would stop by the Kingdom, and I would fix what I could on the broken trucks. I did not have a big inventory on parts because those cost me money and the parts might never be used. I had kept lots of parts in inventory for my semi-trucks and trailers. If my inventory parts fit what was broken, then it was the truck driver's lucky day. The fuel company still owed me money and I was nice to the semi-truck drivers that stopped into the Kingdom hopping I could perform magic. But I would tell them that the big fuel company had to pay their outstanding invoices before I would help them out. The dumbass manager was long gone and the new people in the office did not seem to care about the company semi-trucks broken 1200km in Northern Manitoba. I know if had truck drivers working in the middle of nowhere, arrangements would have been made a head of time for quick and speedy repairs.

The best example of this was on April 21, 2017, I sent Xena to Winnipeg MB to pay for our newly purchased items. The money tree had blossomed very well with OZie money. Xena and I then spent the money foolishly by investing in better equipment for these drill programs on the mineral claims that I had optioned to the OZie. It took about a week to get everything organized for Xena to travel South for the items. Then have Suzan drive her back to the Kingdom in her semi-truck. The money was in my bank account, and we had to travel over the so-called road to Thompson MB. Once in Thompson MB, I had to do the banking and other things so Xena could ride the overnight Greyhound bus to Winnipeg MB. I gave Xena $121,000.00 in bank drafts for the items we had purchased then I gave her $9000.00 in flash cash money. The last thing I wanted on this Southern shopping trip was drama. Xena and I always paid cash for everything, so we know it was paid for. I said goodbye to Xena at the bus depot then I drove back over the so-called road to the Kingdom. Xena had it easy with just riding along on the Greyhound bus while I drove then had to unpack all the supplies and shopping, we did in Thompson MB. When I arrived back in the Kingdom at 3am in the morning, Xena had messaged me on Facebook saying the bus ride was boring. I messaged her back saying I had just arrived home and had to unpack everything. My daughter then messaged back telling me to enjoy unpacking. Oh well, I should have gone to Winnipeg MB instead of her. It was 4:30am in the morning when I had everything put away and enjoying my pain medication Vodka when I messaged Xena that I was done. She replied back that the Greyhound bus will be in Winnipeg MB at 7am which was right on time. Suzan was to meet her at the bus depot then go for breakfast. I messaged Xena goodnight before my pain medication Vodka effected my ability to spell words on the keyboard.

When I woke up at noon, I had to check my messages on Facebook to see how Xena was doing in Winnipeg MB. She was 19-years old with $130,000.00 in money to buy items for us. I just hoped she did not fall in love with some horny toad boy on the Greyhound bus. When I did open my messages on Facebook, there was a picture of Xena and Suzan's husband, the 6'8" tattooed biker that was the manager at the fuel company. Suzan was not back in Winnipeg MB with the semi-truck because she did not get unloaded the day before. One of the joys of driving a semi-truck was nothing every goes according to plan. But her husband was there driving Xena around and helping with the purchases of the items we bought. Now I felt better with a 6'8" tattooed biker helping my daughter out with the $130,000.00 in funds she had. It was later in the day when I got a telephone call from the dealership where I bought the mini-Hoe. I had to buy a mini-Hoe to fly under the helicopter on the drill program to clean up the drill sites. I had bought the mini hoe based on what the helicopter could lift. Now the salesman for the mini-Hoe was calling which I thought was strange. Xena had the bank draft to pay for the machine and was to look it over to make sure the serial numbers were correct. But the salesman was calling to tell me that Thelma & Louise had arrived to pick up my mini-Hoe. I asked the salesman if there was a problem which his reply was that I had sent 2-ladies. "Yes" was my reply because Suzan drives the winter roads with me and Xena knows how to run and chain down a mini-Hoe because that what she did with the big-Hoe at Buddy Barry's shop. Now the salesman was all quiet on the telephone because my name now clicked into his memory that I was on the Ice Road Truckers TV show. Now the salesman said thank you for my business and said goodbye. It was at supper time when Xena messaged me from the Keg steakhouse that they had purchased and loaded ¾ of the semi-truck. Plus, she sent a picture of the new shoes she had bought and told me the colour since I am colour blind. I was glad she told me the colour of her new shoes so I did not have to guess the colour but Xena had grown up all her life with telling me the colours of everything. Plus, Xena sent a picture of Suzan's husband on the mini-Hoe to show how small the mini-Hoe really was. The 6'8" tattooed biker did look funny on the mini-Hoe and the mini-Hoe look like a kid's ride in the mall that required coins for a ride. I said goodbye to Xena on Facebook messenger because I had things to do.

Xean and Suzan left Winnipeg MB early in the morning to travel to The Pas MB to pick my broken quad that had been fixed. The Pas MB was known for the D.O.T. Scale Inspectors for being bad like Dirty Lyle in the film Convoy. The only problem was the D.O.T. Inspector was female and she took a dis-like to Suzan. Suzan and her potty mouth got a couple of pink pieces of paper for trying to make an honest living by driving a semi-truck. The real problem for Suzan was the fact the D.O.T. Inspector had called ahead to Thompson MB to say that Suzan would be arriving. The Thompson MB D.O.T. Inspector was also female which was not in Suzan's favor. But Suzan did not care, her and Xena continued on with picking up the items in The Pas MB then heading to Thompson MB. Just South of town, the D.O.T. Inspector was waiting and pulled Suzan's semi-truck over and the lady was rude right from the moment she opened her mouth. Xena sat, watched and learned at how D.O.T. Inspector show no mercy because it was a cash grab for the government. When it had ended, Suzan got a few more pink pieces of paper to add to her collection. Xena had used the pay-as-you-go cell phone to call the Sportsman Dealership where they were to pick up the new Quads for the drill program. The Sportsman Dealership said they would wait for them to arrive to load the semi-truck. Xena was thinking ahead like I had raised her to think and if she had not called the dealership then they might not have gotten loaded. With the last of the items loaded in Thompson MB, Xena called to say they were leaving Thompson MB. But she called back 10-minutes later to say they were on the side of the road North of Thompson MB. The D.O.T. Inspector had pulled Suzan over again because now they are saying Suzan did not have enough hours left in her "logbook" to legally drive to WHO-ville. Xena kept talking on the pay-as-you-go cell phone to tell me what was happening between the 2-ladies arguing outside the semi-truck. Suzan told the D.O.T. Inspector that she had enough hours to legally drive through to WHO-ville if the D.O.T. Inspectors had not wasted 4-hours of her day. The best part was when Xena told me that Suzan told the D.O.T. Inspector that she was going to WHO-ville. There was a motel room waiting for her plus her pain medication from having to deal with the D.O.T. Inspectors. That was when Xena told me that Suzan was back in the semi-truck, and they will be in the Kingdom in 4-hours. I was so glad Suzan did not stay in Thompson MB with all our new purchases on the deck of the semi-trailer. Thompson MB was known for a high crime rate so the odds of our new purchases still being on the semi-trailer in the morning would be very slim. When Suzan and Xena arrived in the Kingdom 4-hours later, I gave both a ride in the pink crew cab. We dropped Suzan off at the motel so she could relax, and I dropped Xena off at her house. Xena had all the receipts and paperwork organized for the $130,000.00 she had spent in 2-days on the Southern trip for her. Plus, she liked the new shoes she had bought too.

In the morning we unloaded our new purchases from Suzan's semi-trailer then reloaded it with goodies to go South. Suzan relaxed in the motel room until we were finished loading. She wanted to be fully rested so she could travel straight through to Winnipeg MB. But time it correctly to pass through Thompson MB when the government D.O.T. Inspectors were gone for the day. Now the Kingdom had some nice new fun toys as we called them which the mini-Hoe was the most popular. The $40,000.00 machine was handy to have working on the cats for lifting the pieces or cleaning the snow off the walkways. Plus, people also had a good laugh at how small the mini-Hoe was that was not a toy. The machine was well engineered and had lots of power for its size which made it even more fun.

Since the OZie drill program paid us every month not like anything we did on the winter roads or in repairs that took forever to get paid or not paid at all. We decided to take the summer off from working for other people but still work on our collectables in the Kingdom. One of my Facebook friends at the time was part of the TV show Highway through Hell. This fellow we will call Max, wanted to film a TV show called the King of Obsolete, but he was not the big Hollywood. He was just a guy with a bunch of cameras that wanted to film a pilot show then marketed it to the Hollywood Gods. Xena and I both agreed to this because we did like the 15 seconds of fame, we had with Ice Road Truckers. But the Hollywood Gods never did anything more with us for some reason because we thought it was, we were Canadian. Max wanted to fly from Toronto ON right through to Thompson MB. Then rent a car to drive over the so-called road to the Kingdom. I advised him not to fly past Winnipeg MB and rent a nice SUV to drive the 1200kms to the end of the world. Max agreed to what I had suggested because he priced everything out and the costs was over ½ price if he had flown to Thompson MB and rented a vehicle. Anything to do with traveling North, the costs are double. Plus, I also pointed out that Max had all his camera equipment and luggage. The offspring of Cheech and Chong working at the Northern airline company, they will lose all the luggage for sure. Then he would lose a day or "2" in Thompson MB waiting for his luggage to arrive. This had happened too many times in the past because there was no customer service with the Northern airlines. With all arrangement made, Max will arrive in the Kingdom Thursday night before the Canadian long weekend in August. As Max traveled, he was very concerned because no one at the motel had returned his emails or telephone calls. Xena and I assured Max that that was normal because there was no customer service in WHO-ville. Xena stopped by when there was staff at the motel to get Max checked in, so we had the room key when he arrived. We were so used to WHO-ville that we tried to control as much as we could because we wanted repeat customers and film crews too.

Max kept us posted as he traveled and arrived in the Kingdom at 7pm on Thursday night. Of course, Max was a film guy, and this was his project that he was marketing to make "us" famous and "him" rich. Max got the film camera out right away and began filming the minute he arrived in the Kingdom. I was so glad I did not have any of my pain medication Vodka before he arrived, I was on my best behavior. We hit it off well because Max was a Canadian and wanted to show Northern Canada like it really was not through the eyes of Hollywood. Also, Max was laid back in his filming and wanted all natural not Hollywood drama that everyone sees on TV. With the long days of daylight in the Kingdom, we got a lot of film footage shot on the first day. When it was too dark to shoot any film, Max headed to the motel because he was still on a different time zone plus, he made the trip all in one day including the 1200km drive to the end of the world. The next day I drove Max around WHO-ville so he could see the town and the people that hated me so much. For filming the King of Obsolete TV show, the film crews would have to stay in WHO-ville for 3-weeks at a time then switch out. The film crew could not stay any longer because the mental issues of being at the end of the world. Then my TV show would have to include Dr. Fraser Crane as a regular so the film crew and everyone else involved could get mental health help. I left the South after the DIEvorce and fit in well in the Great White North, but I knew I would not fit in if I moved back South. Then I would be the one seeing Dr. Fraser Crane on a daily basis. As we drove around, Max could not get over all the brand-new vehicles parked at the run-down houses for being an old mining town. Max came from Toronto and lives in the suburbs where everyone works hard to have nice cars and nice houses. But in WHO-ville welfare was a source of income and the new car dealers handed out cars to everyone except me. I went to the GM dealer in Thompson MB with $5000.00 to put down on a new "gas" power truck to replace the "diesel" powered pink crew cab. The salesman was very nice to me and showed me the door which I then drove my pink crew cab off the dealership lot. Being the King of Obsolete on national TV around the world. Also, a small business owner for a long time with $5000.00 in my hand did not qualified me for any new vehicle that was on the dealership lot. Now if I was on welfare and had 7-kids which the government of Canada rewarded me on the 19th of every month with up to $500.00 per kid. Then I would have been driving a new car off the dealership lot with no questions asked. But I did point out to Max, that all the mines are closed and there was no work. If it was not for welfare, the WHO-ville hospital would not be busy plus the airport had airplanes everyday which were medivacs to fly people out who are sick. Max agreed that there was a trade off on having the welfare which means people living in the North and the town of WHO-ville was barely surviving.

After stopping and visiting most of the businesses in WHO-ville so Max could get an idea what it would be like to live here for a year while filming. I saved the best place for last which was the new gold company saying they were going to start gold mining in WHO-ville again. The person in charge of the WHO-ville operation lived on the west coast like all the other employees they fly into WHO-ville. I had warned Max about this fellow and told him that I was standing with a group of people outside the café and this fellow introduced everyone in the group except for me to the government official. The government official that had flown up to WHO-ville to see the work in progress but knew me through the mining convention and TV show fame. To me it did not bother me that the fellow did not introduce me because it made him look like the real "asshole" he really was. The people in the group felt bad for me and apologized afterwards for not being introduce. My reply back to the people in the group was I only got 15 seconds of fame around the world and if I only got 16 seconds then I would have got introduced. Max has his film camera ready as we meet everyone in the gold mining office. I explained that Max was here to film a pilot TV show for me to get my own show that will be filmed over a year. It was the same speech I gave at all the other places and business which everyone thought would be good for WHO-ville. The Ice Road Truckers show was filmed with me was good marketing for WHO-ville and around the world with lots of re-runs too. Once I was done my speech the fellow in charge the gold operations went in to a 10-minute-long rant how he would never hire me or have anything to do with me. Everyone in the room included me was very surprised at what came out of this fellow's mouth. Max even moved his head away from viewing the film camera to look at me to see if this was a real act or maybe a comedy. When the fellow was done his rant, Max and I just turned and walked out of the building. I was not really surprised at the fellow being an asshole towards me, but he should have held back his hatred for me to smile and market the gold project.

As Max and I drive to Eldon Lake to visit the float airplane base, it was Max who talked about the hatred that fellow had for me. I told him I was nice to them when they came to WHO-ville in 2015 and I helped them out. But I guess the locals who hated me, convinced the new gold people to hate me like everyone else. When we arrived at the water base, the float airplanes are all there which means the manager will be there to chat with us. The manager was female and was very good at promoting the airplanes for filming the King of Obsolete show. That would mean work for her and the other employees that are getting less and less flying each year. The American Fishing Lodges were losing customers each year with the new rules for cdn-usa border crossings. As we chatted with the manager, she enjoyed a cigarette because once done chatting with us she was flying to deliver some freight to a lodge. It was an excellent visit, and the manager really promoted the flying company and stayed focused on what Max needed to hear to bring in the big Hollywood money. On the drive back to the Kingdom, I asked Max if he noticed that the manager was a pilot, and he did not understand my question. I then told max while we chatted, the manager enjoyed a cigarette because she would not be able to smoke in the airplane. But she had a drink from her water bottle which she put between her legs to remove the twist cap then took a drink. Once she was done drinking, she put the water bottle back between her legs to put the twist cap back on. Anyone smoking a cigarette would have used the hand holding the cigarette. The manager was a true pilot doing everything one hand like she would do flying the airplane. Max then reviewed the film footage he took on his camera as I drove the pink crew cab. He then agreed when he seen the manager on film and paid attention to her doing everything one handed like a camera man filming to get the footage. Back in the Kingdom we did more filming and Max got out his drone for the detailed fun shots. The days of filming with a helicopter were long gone because the $6000.00 drone camera were state of the art. The only hard part for us was the drone sounded like a big mosquito as it buzzed around Xena and I for Max to get the film footage he wanted. As Max and I enjoyed a booze beverage in the house, I was checking Facebook to see what my Kingdom Followers were up too. Max had to use the internet to check in back home before his kids went to bed. One of my Kingdom Followers in Kinoosao SK was on Facebook say the forest fire had just started due to a lightning strike from a thunderstorm that came through town. Now this post on Facebook concerned me because in the morning we were taking Max and the boat to Kinoosao. As Max and I enjoyed the booze beverage, the post of the forest fire by Kinoosao was getting lots of replies. Which most of them were saying the original poster was a drama queen with the forest fire not even being close to Kinoosao. When Max had enough booze beverage for the evening, he returned to his motel room. We agreed that in the morning we would find out more on the forest fire by Kinoosao.

In the morning, the posts on the fire by Kinoosao were no better because the in the darkness between 1am to 4am, the glow of the forest fire really showed the location and how close it was to the community. Max and I decide to drive to Kinoosao without the boat or any of the under-water Mermaid searching equipment. It was not worth the risk in being trapped up on Reindeer Lake if the forest fire was that close to the community. Xena decided not to join us on the boring trip over the Kinoosao Rally Road. Max had set up Go-Pros to get film footage of the Kinoosao Rally Road plus I had to wear a microphone to record the boring trip. After 3.5-hours of traveling the 100kms to Kinoosao, even Max was saying the road was unforgiven. But we did get a lot of film footage with me speaking to point out the details and points of interest. We did stop at lookout point to see the damage done to the toothpick trees and pieces of the film chase car that were smashed up when we filmed for the TV show Ice Road Truckers. It was the day I missed km66.6 Number of the Beast corner or famously known as Ricochet Hill. Max was very surprised that the film chase car even tried passing the semi-truck driven by the actor. But the actor told the film chase car on the radio to pass because it was all good. The rest of the drive to Kinoosao impressed Max because the Kinoosao Rally Road showed no mercy. When we arrived at the top of the big hill going into Kinoosao, we stopped so Max could send his drone camera over to see the forest fire. The fellow posting on Facebook was correct with the forest fire being right close. Max flew his drone back to us at the pink crew cab then told me that we could not stay long in Kinoosao. What Max had seen on the drone camera showed the forest fire close to the community like the fellow posting on Facebook and he did not have a drone. It was a short drive down the big hill which Max even thought it was very steep then to turn 90-dregrees to cross a small narrow bridge. I told Max that it was even more fun sliding backwards down the hill then trying not to miss the small narrow bridge. Max replied back that it would be good filming. Now that made me smile because all those years of trying to conquer the big hill, I could have used a film crew.

When arriving in Kinoosao, the first place to go was the Co-op Store because that was the local hub of activity. Today was no different but more people were there because of the concerns of the forest fire. Max was first to show everyone the film footage from the drone camera which surprised a lot of people. The fellow on Facebook was correct and the community of Kinoosao will be evacuated very soon. I purchased my usual candy bars and Pepsi from the Co-op Store to support the business. Max did the same as the people watched the film footage from the drone over and over. We decided not to stay long in Kinoosao because the last thing we wanted was to be trapped there till the forest fire was over. We said goodbye to everyone and left the community which was a very short visit. The pink crew cab climbed the steep hill, and the rear tires would slip once in a while to get traction on the big hill because it was so steep. When the rear tires slipped, Max looked at me and smiled because he knew that the filming would be great on this big hill in the summer or winter time. As we drove, we could see the forest fire burning in the toothpick trees alongside the Kinoosao Rally Road. I had to drive the road with speed which meant 1-foot on the brake and 1-foot on the gas pedal. I could not let fear and common sense hold me back with the forest fire right beside the road. Once passed the main fire area, we had to deal with the thick smoke that was worse than a London Fog to see the road. Plus, it was hard to breath as we drove along the Kinoosao Rally Road. When we were 50kms from Kinoosao and stopped at the start of the winter road for Max to fly the drone again. I thanked Max for bringing the drone and flying it over the forest fire, so we knew the situation and told the people of Kinoosao. If we did not have the drone film footage, we would not have known how bad or how close the forest fires were. If we had stayed in Kinoosao being social butterflies, then the forest fire would have crossed the Kinoosao Rally Road trapping us in the community. Max told me, no problem for helping out plus he got the film footage from the drone to be used in other projects he was working on.

At the start of the winter road, Max could not believe that the winter road was all muskeg with lots of water sitting on top. As Max flew the drone around, I told him the winter road was all muskeg for the first 3kms because the government built the road in 1998. The drone Max had was used for filming on other TV shows and could travel a great distance away from him operating it. I then told Max to follow the trail through the toothpick trees that was on high ground. The drone did that and we watched what it was recording on the little TV screen. Max could not believe the government started a winter road in wet muskeg when there was good high ground right beside the wet muskeg. "Yes" only the government did stupid things and keeps doing it year after year. Max asked if we used the good trail beside the winter road when conditions are bad, and I told him "yes". It was our ace card up our sleeve like a good gambler when the conditions were impassable on the winter road with wet muskeg. When Max had enough film footage with the drone, we headed back to the Kingdom to do more filming. I had used the satellite phone to let Xena know that we would be back early for more filming. When we did arrive back in the Kingdom, the posts on Facebook were of the people of Kinoosao being evacuated by boat on Reindeer Lake. With the forest fire blocking off the Kinoosao Rally Road that we had just traveled. The people of Kinoosao spent 3-weeks away from home because of the forest fire but no damage to the community. Now if we had not left the community when we did, our escape would be by boat too. After escaping by boat, we would have had to travel to Brochet MB to buy airplane tickets to Thompson MB. If and when we arrived in Thompson MB because no plans could be made. Xena would have had to drive to over the so-called road to pick us for us to return to the Kingdom. That would have made for good filming but cost a lot of money too. We are so glad we listened to the fellow on Facebook that was making the correct updates on his posts. When Xena came to the Kingdom, and Max and I were sitting inside the house. The first thing Xena said was "we smelled of smoke". She then checked the pink crew cab which smelled of forest fire smoke. Max and I did not notice the smell of smoke because we could still taste it in our mouths. Plus, we really smelled bad but the amount of smoke we breathed in to drive beside the fire lasted forever in our noses.

After filming the rest of the day, Max returned to his motel room and will leave in the morning to head back to Winnipeg MB. Max wanted to film Suzan in Winnipeg MB because she would be driving the winter roads with us on my TV show. We got busy in the Kingdom and only chatted with Suzan and Max on Facebook to find out the filming went well with her and her semi-truck in Winnipeg MB. The next time we heard from Max was for a big conference call with the Hollywood Gods in Hollywood. The conference call went excellent, and everyone was impressed that I could talk and make long sentences since I rode the short bus to school. The last we heard from Max was on a conference call with him saying he was going to send us Go-Pro cameras. This was to get more test film footage on the winter drill road season which had us building these roads. Nothing arrived and Max never popped up on Facebook or anywhere else. I guess Max became Hollywood and only needed us to better his career and disappeared. Oh well, there will be other Hollywood filming for Xena and me.

## Chapter 4
**KoO-Tracks**


One of the purchases we made that day back in April 2017 when Xena went to Winnipeg MB with $131,000.00 in fun money. I had bought a set of used rubber tracks that bolt on where the wheels of the vehicle go. These were to be the greatest thing since sliced beard for people to get out and enjoy the Great White North in the comfort of their 4x4 vehicle. I did not care about driving to cruise Dairy Queen to see and be seen, I wanted the individual tracks to break up the non-frozen muskeg to get it to freeze when building winter roads. The fellow I bought the rubber tracks from had a little problem with them when he decided to travel to his cabin across the frozen lake. The one-track set caught the slush on the frozen lake to "flip up" and jam against the body of his Jeep. "Yes", when the body of the "Jeep" got damaged. The rubber tracks were removed quickly like my name was removed on the mortgage papers for "my" house after the DIEvorce. Then the rubber tracks sat sitting and I offered to buy the rubber tracks which the fellow warned me that they are known to "flip up". I assured the fellow that I had a welder and the "flip up" would be corrected. I also had a 2001 Chevy 4x4 truck that was well rusted out on the body. The Chevy truck could never pass a vehicle inspection to be registered on the Manitoba roads. The Manitoba roads may not be safe to travel on but the government wanted all vehicles to be safe for traveling on the non-safe roads.

I phoned the manufacturing in the USA to chat about making the rubber tracks from the Jeep fit the Chevy truck. All it took was my credit card getting whacked for $2600.00 cdn money and the parts were sent to the end of the world. I had told the manufacture in the USA that I was famous for 15 seconds on national TV and I wanted these rubber tracks to be mounted and done correctly. The last thing I wanted was the rubber tracks to fall apart while filming "my" TV show. The fellow sent me all the info and was very helpful in getting everything done correctly because this was free marketing for the manufacture. When all the parts arrived for mounting the rubber tracks on the Chevy truck, I could not believe that the brackets did not bolt up and a few other things. By the time I was done welding and hammering to make the rubber tracks from a Jeep fit the Chevy I could have done it all myself in the Kingdom using recycled scrap metal like all my other projects. The $2600.00 whacked on my credit card could have been spent foolish on my ex-fiancé with expensive sexy outfit for her to wear and for me to remove. When I did get the rubber tracks on the Chevy, I went for a test drive around the Kingdom in the muddy dirt since it was the end of the month of May. Next Xena helped me load the Chevy truck with the rubber tracks on to the new leased trailer. The true test drive will be on the mineral claims South of WHO-ville. As we drove through WHO-ville in the pink crew cab towing the new leased trailer, everyone was looking and waving at us. The Chevy truck with rubber tracks was something the locals did not see every day. At the mineral claims, we unloaded the Chevy truck for the test drive on the winter drill roads that had melted away. Like my Honeymoon the test drive was over in 10-minutes with a 1-hour walk back to the pink crew cab sitting on the road back to WHO-ville. We were not happy campers having to walk on the wet ground and the bugs were bad. I killed 1-bug and 1000-showed up for the funeral which drove us nuts as we walked out to the road.

Now we had to go back to the Kingdom and get a small cat to drag the broken Chevy truck to the road to load it on the new leased trailer for the trip back to the Kingdom. The small cat had no problems and the tracks never fell apart with the cat being close to 80-years old. Back in the Kingdom, I ripped the rubber tracks off the Chevy truck and tossed them in the shop. I had taken lots of pictures to show the manufacture in the USA what a quality product they had made, and I had bought. It was only 10-minutes after I sent the politely worded email to the manufacture in the USA that I got a nasty email back with the words of "our lawyer" being used. The rubber tracks they had sold me had never worked for the fellow with the Jeep and now they did not work for me, and the manufacture said it was my fault. The nasty email basically stated that I should have never left the paved parking lot at Dairy Queen to drive off-road with these off-road tracks set up. I had just spent $14,000.00 for a 10-minute ride like my Honeymoon and now I was getting blamed it was my fault the rubber tracks fell apart. Just like my Honeymoon it was my fault, and this was only costing more money to correct. Since the rubber track manufacture was not being nice and wanting for their product to work in Canada, I now had to make them work. In my wasted youth living in the South, I worked for a fertilizer company that designed and built rubber belt conveyors. These use-less design of rubber tracks were the same as any conveyors I had designed or built. It was a long 50-hours of welding and fixing to make the rubber tracks the KoO-Tracks. Once back on the Chevy truck, we did the test driving around the Kingdom but had to wait until the winter snows came in October.

(pink crew cab towing the new leased trailer)

In October the snows came, and the KoO-Tracks got used regularly to pack the snow down on the winter drill roads. My improvements made these the perfect rubber tracks in the Great White North. The KoO-Tracks could break through the thin frozen crust on the muskeg to bring up the water to make the muskeg freeze. Plus, the KoO-Tracks Chevy truck was "cool" to drive, and everyone liked seeing it on the new leased trailer as we hauled it back and forth to the Kingdom after day of fun. Then the big test was on November 12, 2017, when we hauled the KoO-Tracks to the start of the winter road on the Kinoosao Rally Road. The snow never stopped and the grader snowplowed snowbanks on the Kinoosao Rally Road were very high for being the start of winter. We took our time traveling the Kinoosao Rally Road because today was relaxing day for us and all we needed was film footage and pictures. When we arrived at the start of the winter road, the snow in the ditch covering the deep water was not even frozen.

(the water in the ditch was not frozen)

We usually unloaded the new leased trailer then back the trailer into the start of the winter road and then drive away in the pink crew cab with the everything facing the way we came. But not this year, we had to unhook the new leased trailer then turn the pink crew cab around on the narrow road.

To turn around it took about 50-forwards and backups to get the vehicle turned around so we could then hook a chain on the new leased trailer to spin it around. That was the part of survival in the Great White North always make sure the vehicle was point in the direction of home because if we broke down and had to walk back to the pink crew cab. Then to try and turn around in the dark only to get stuck we might not survive. With everything hooked back up and ready to travel back to WHO-ville when we came off the winter road. It was now time to have fun and get the film and pictures required.

(KoO-Tracks performing well in the snow)

The KoO-Tracks could not cross the ditch to be on the winter road because of the water. If the KoO-Tracks got stuck, we did not have anything to pull or winch it out. Now we had to go back down the Kinoosao Rally Road 1/2km to the high ground in the toothpick trees. There was a series of trails that traveled beside the winter road because the government had built the start of the winter road in the muskeg not on good ground. The snow was too deep for Xena to break trail with her ski-doo, so I had to do it with the KoO-Tracks which worked out good. Once I found the trail down to the winter road, it was easy to just arrive on the winter road. I had no idea how "un-frozen" the winter road was because it was like driving on a rolling wave in a boat. The KoO-Tracks broke through everywhere with water coming up on the rubber tracks as I drove along with great speed.

(climbing up off the winter road, toothpick trees)

There was way too much snow on the winter road, and I knew the Brochet road crew would have great problems trying to open the winter roads starting December 01 in Brochet MB. Xena was able to get a lot of good film footage and good pictures for marketing. When we were done having fun, it was a quick drive through the toothpick trees back to the waiting pink crew cab.

(loaded up and heading back to the Kingdom)

Everything went perfect and we were back in WHO-ville to have burgers and fries at the Dead Barn Café. We parked the pink crew cab out front and cross the street so we could watch everyone drive by and look at the KoO-Tracks. The pictures and film were a great success on my website and on Facebook. The KoO-Track Chevy truck got painted black with the paint brush and roller to match everything else in the Kingdom. As the snow came, we kept packing the winter drill roads for the drill program that was starting in January 2018. The Brochet road crew struggled to get the winter road open, but the deep snow was making it very hard for them. This was the second year in a row that the snow was deep and the ground not frozen. Plus, the government was not offering any money or help because the government does not want businesses being successful. It was near the end of January when the Brochet road crew had the winter road open which was 6-weeks later than usual for them.

I chatted with the Brochet road crew foreman at the cardlock, and he asked why I did not pack the winter road up farther then I did. I told him we went up there to get film footage and pictures, but it turned out we had packed the start of the winter road very well. The tracks from the KoO-Tracks had packed the snow down and the water flowed up to surface to freeze. The 3kms of fun we had that day made it so easy for the Brochet road crew to just plow the road open like any other year. I did point out to the foreman that Xena and I had started packing our winter drill roads in October so they would freeze well plus we kept packing as the snows came. The foreman told me the government would pay any extra to employ people to ski-doo pack and work the snow as it fell. The government wanted us all on welfare instead of working and bettering ourselves. I agreed with the foreman because the only staff I had was my daughter because no one wanted to work anymore because welfare paid too good. The KoO-Tracks served us well with over 1900km driven on them that winter and no problems. On numerous Google searches on the manufactured rubber tracks out of the USA, I never seen any worn-out rubber track sets for sale. All the ones that were for sale were brand new in the storage shed or on the ground where they were removed. They are the worst product I have ever had in my life and not sure how the manufacture keeps selling a non-working product. Looking back, I should just build my own KoO-Tracks because it would have been cheaper and less stress.

## Chapter 5
**Terrible Year**


The year 2018 started off to be a good year with Xena and I supposed to be getting our own TV show. The mineral claims I had optioned to the OZie were supposed to pay very well with working being done. But every time we think we will hitting the big time and not have to work as hard; the dreams all fall apart. Max who came up and filmed us on the August long weekend in 2017 just disappeared like Jimmy Hoffa with no communication or anything about the TV show King of Obsolete. The only problem was I had signed a 1-year contract with Max to look in to marketing us. The contract was like my marriage contract which meant that the one party could do anything they wanted but me. Max could disappear with no communication and if I talked or tried to market myself to bring in a source of income. Then Max would pop up like an ex-wife or Revenue Canada wanting part of the money. I had spent enough money on lawyers over the years that I could have went to law school myself. I decided just to sit tight and behave until the 1-year contract was up in October 2018. The last thing I needed was a lawyer and court appearances which require me to clean up and look presentable for the judge. But the day Max re-appears in my life like an ex-wife, he will find out I am English with a very good memory. The Ozies were not very generous with the money in 2018 with Xena and I building the drill roads in the deep snow that cause the ground not to be frozen. But Xena and I do good quality work and did not worry what the OZies thought or if they were going to pay all my invoices in full because I had optioned my mineral claims to them, so I had the last laugh in theory. The OZies also hired out the "playing of the drill core" to a company in Yellowknife NWT. Now I had these young stuck up university kids running around the Kingdom making demands because they could not organize a "piss up at a brewery". The best one was at 5pm on a Sunday, one of the young kids knocked on my door to chew me an asshole about some pallets of core. The young kid was not very smart because he was standing on my doorstep, on my property and it was Sunday. At my age I did not care if I ever seen the young kid ever again because he was dumb enough to be the manager in the next couple of years and that was when I told him to "F**K OFF" and get off my property. The OZies did not like me standing up for myself and I should be nice to people who chew me an asshole on a Sunday on my property. That was when I knew my days were number with OZies because the drill program had turned in to nothing but greed.

We did not have any winter road customers because we were only dealing with companies that paid their invoices, I had sent them. The fuel company still owed me money for the last 2-years with no interest in paying or even talking about why I would not fix the broken semi-trucks. The truck drivers for the fuel company would stop in the Kingdom at the start of the winter road season to get FREE King of Obsolete goodies and girlie calendars. But I would never see them again or get offered a FREE coffee or a meal at the café uptown. Once again, I am the Bride's Maid with them only knowing me when they wanted something. In March, just past the Kingdom, they had a loaded fuel tanker semi-truck end up in the ditch on its side. When I heard about the accident, I drove out the accident site to see if they needed my help. When I arrived, there was 6-truck drivers there pumping the fuel off. I walked up to them, and they all turned their backs to me to ignore me. Now that pissed me off because all 6-truck drivers had been in my house eating my food, drinking my beer and using my pink crew cab to get around town while I had fixed their broken semi-trucks. I then turned around and walked back to the pink crew cab to drive back to the Kingdom. Most people would have been upset with these people turning their back to me, but I was used to it. My own family did it to me when I turned 18-years old, and I was driving my 37 Dodge hot rod truck with Naughty Natalie. We arrived at a family function only to be turned away which I wrote about in my 6th book Love is Trust which is the 2nd book in the Naughty Natalie Book Series. I viewed these people turning their back on me as very narrow-minded people who think they are better than me. I have always lived my life treating people the way I wanted to be treated. I know the fuel tanker accident cost a lot of money compared to any of the accidents I was involved with in the clean up over the 12-years we did business with the fuel company.

By the end of March, the Ozie drill program ended with us being owed a lot of money. Then the government winter roads closed and there were no job offers for running over the winter roads when closed with the last of the freight. The only things that was our income in the Kingdom was repairing the broken equipment for the first nation community. The community got a new manager that did not like everything being shipped South to be repaired. I was now fixing everything which required a lot of thinking better known as "thought" because the people at the community seemed to break everything. They did not understand how things worked. I went from being the King of Obsolete to owning code readers to figure the complex reasons why the new style equipment quit or was broken. It was great fun learning and learning more to be one step ahead of the breakage. The big project for me was when a 1996 Chevy 1-ton truck ended up in the lake which I think they were trying to wash the truck and the interior. I was able to recover the truck and get it up and running. I had years of experience working on my sunken cats that went swimming. The money was paying the bills and it was a good retirement job which I was starting to like. The last couple of years doing winter road repairs and work did not pay very well with lots of money still owed. Xena and I were glad when 2018 ended because 2019 was going to be a better year with maybe our own TV show or the YouTube videos we had been making would become popular.

## Chapter 6
## Non Payment Trip

Xena and I were glad when the year 2019 had arrived because it was going to be a better year. The January temperatures were extra cold, and we were glad that we were not building winter drill roads. The fall freeze was not the greatest, but we did not get the deep snow like we did for the past 2-years. The Brochet road crew built their part of the winter road from Brochet MB to the Kinoosao Rally Road but had a late start. The Brochet road crew always started December 01 every year to try and have the winter road open for the community members to travel South to buy Xmas presents. But in 2019 they never got started until December 20 because the government was being cheap. The government wanted all winter roads built from tree to tree wide and plowed to the dirt. For the last 20-years the contractors plowed open the roads to let it freeze then worked the snow to make a nice road base and only plowed the winter road 4-Caterpillar dozer blades wide. Now the government wanted the winter road plowed tree to tree which can make it 8-Caterpillar dozer blades wide. Plus plowing the winter road to the dirt meant that all the rocks will be found by the blades of the dozers which will cause breakage. The reason why the government was cheap and really cheaped out by making the contractors do 3-times as much work on the road break for the same amount of money. All other years the contractors opened the winter road then they got paid to maintenance with dragging and finish touches with the road graders. The government was saving money which costed us money and I knew the winter roads would melt away before the government officially closed them near the end of March. The winter roads had always been a road base of hard packed snow that was layers of ice. These made for strong roads that did not melt away and we could still drive on white snow packed road near the end of April 2014. Now the new government cheap winter roads will just melt away and the communities will lose access to the outside world sooner. The contractor that built most of the best roads took his equipment home when the government wrote in the contracts what the new winter roads will be like and no cost plus or extras. The contractor was smart but several of his employees who had been employed over the years decided they could build the winter road to Tadoule MB on the money the government was offering. When employees think they can run the company better and decided to start their own company to build winter roads. That was when I was very cautious with any business dealings. Employees are employees and figure they can do better until it was time to run the business with most failing. The employees were my new best friends and made me promises and promises of all this work I was going to get fixing their equipment up the winter roads. I reminded them several times that I was working my retirement job fixing broken new style equipment that paid very well. But I was not going to leave them high and dry when it came time to repair an important piece of equipment.

My new best friends were in and out of the Kingdom needing this and needing that. Once they headed up the winter roads to begin building the winter road from km160 to km338 which was Tadoule MB. My new best friends then called me on the satellite phone to get advice or parts sent up. The only problem, the only winter road that was open was to Brochet MB and the road branched off the main winter road to Tadoule MB. Any parts or supplies I had sent up to my new best friends by the winter road semi-trucks hauling to Brochet MB would drop the items on the snowbank under the Brochet Junction turn off sign. Then my new best friends would drive down the non-open winter road to pick up the items they needed. This all sounded easy on paper, but it was a nightmare. The semi-truck carrying the items might break down or the truck driver would forget to drop off the item at the sign. My new best friends would arrive at the Brochet Junction sign to find no items left for them. Then they would call me all excited that they had just traveled 5-hours on the rough winter road to find nothing. I would then tell them what semi-truck I had given the items too and they could use the FM Radio to call out to see if anyone was around for 20-miles. Usually, the items were close by and arrived just after my new best friends called me all excited. Sometimes the truck driver would forget to drop the items off at the Brochet Junction sign then drop the items off at the next mile marker sign. Then the truck driver would tell my new best friends on the FM Radio where the items were located. This was the only system that worked to get parts and supplies up the winter roads. Plus, it worked a lot better than any cargo aviation company based in Thompson MB who had the offspring of Cheech and Chong working for them.

Then at 3pm while I was having a coffee in the house and enjoying the pictures my ex-fiancé had emailed. She was always teasing me with sexy outfit pictures and telling me the wrong colours of the outfits. Being colour blind, she was just trying to screw me up because I know for a fact that a sexy outfit in Big Bird "yellow" would not be very sexy to a non-colour blind person. But for me it was a different shade of grey in my colour blind eyes. Plus, she was the lead cop at the town next to the Kingdom. So, if I liked the sexy outfit, she might, and I mean "might" drive over to visit me in the Kingdom. As I was picking which "yellow" outfit was the sexiest for her to wear for me. The telephone rang which my call display on the telephone showed it as a satellite phone. I answered the telephone, and it was my new best friends calling because they broke the D6 Caterpillar dozer. They are all excited because the blade broke when they hit a rock hidden in the snow on the winter road. That did not surprise me because the government was making the contractors plow the winter roads to the dirt instead of leaving 6" of snow for the road drags to smooth out the road base to hide the rocks. Now for the next 2-hours my new best friends called me on the telephone to give me all the details of what broke on the blade of the dozer. They assured me over and over it was the angle cylinder mounting bracket on the side of the dozer blade. This was a common place where the dozer blades break when finding rocks hidden in the deep snow. Now I had to pack up the welder and tools in the pink crew cab to drive up the winter road at 4am in the morning. My ex-fiancé was mad at me again because I had to go to work and make money instead of spending quality time with her wearing a "yellow" sexy outfit. I did point out to my ex-fiancé who was the cop, how many times she was a "no" show for cuddling on the couch. Just because someone got "shot" and she had to handle all the details right now and left me on the couch. But that was OK because she was a woman and the cop whereas I am a man and my job of fixing broken junk did not matter. Now I see why she was my "ex"-fiancé because we just could not get along.

(Brochet Junction at the closed sign)

In the morning, I had left at 4am so I would arrive at the broken D6 Caterpillar while there was still day light to begin the welding on the simple repair. The Kinoosao Rally Road was perfect to drive and the 108kms up the winter road to the Brochet Junction was perfect too. Then I arrived at the start of where the Southern contractor was building the 50kms to the Lac Brochet Junction which was km160. This part of the winter road was not opened and blocked off to keep the tourist from traveling the non-finished road at -35c. As I drove this part of the winter road, I took lots of pictures of the equipment used and how the winter road was being built in case I ever wrote a book on winter roads. The Southern contractor could not be making money because the amount of equipment and men from the South he had working on the winter road was unreal. Plus, the winter road was plowed tree to tree and to the dirt. By the time the Southern contractor arrived at Lac Brochet MB after 4-weeks work.

(tire drag, farm tractor meaning Southern contractor)

His equipment and men had built a winter road to Lac Brochet MB 6-times by the amount of passes to plow an extra wide winter road. Then to plow the winter road to the dirt like the government wanted meant the contractor had a lot of broken equipment from finding all the rocks hidden in the deep snow on the winter road. I just drove along and shook my head at the waste of money and time by the government trying to save money. The dead giveaway for being a Southern contractor building the winter road was the farm tractor pulling a tire drag. The tire drags work well in the south but not over the rocks and more rocks of these winter roads. Oh well, I just smiled and waved at the fellow driving the farm tractor as if he was back on the farm in the South.

(Southern contractor's camp at km160)

At km160, the Southern contractor had his big camp set up for all his Southern workers. I took a few pictures and continued on up the Tadoule MB winter road to km180. That was where the broken D6 Caterpillar dozer was with my new best friend's small little camp trailer.

(freshly plowed winter road to the broken D6 Cat)

When I arrived, the D6 Caterpillar was not running. But the young kids in camp assured me they would have it up and running so I could weld on the dozer blade. I stood beside the D6 Caterpillar dozer as the one kid cranked over the motor which turned very slowly. It was only -32c and the machine should have never been shut off even if it was broken or not. The electric block heaters on these new style cats are made for the Southern cold weather not the extreme cold weather of the Great White North. Plus, these new style cats are all oil driven for everything and the oils will be thick syrup. But the young kids assured me they will get the D6 Caterpillar running that would not crank over fast enough for the motor to even attempt to start. When the other young kid got the can of ether starting fluid out to make the engine come to life and spray most of the ether can into the air cleaner. That was when I told them to stop before the motor blows up with the amount of ether that was sprayed into the air cleaner. Plus, the young kids were just killing the batteries which would only freeze when dead being this cold out.

(heat of the day meaning D6 Cat was not starting)

I then looked at the angle blade cylinder bracket on the side of the blade that needed to be welded. It was not broken but the young kid pointed to the main blade pivot bushing on the blade that was broken. As I looked at this pivot bushing that had been "bubblegum" welded. I showed the young kids that my welding rods do not fit in to even weld or how do I grind or remove the "bubblegum" welds. The blade of the cat had to come off and should have been sent to me to be welded in my heated little shop. Plus, when I found out who actually owned the D6 Caterpillar dozer that was going to be paying my invoice. The pivot bushing was not fixed properly before being shipped up on the winter road. The owner still owed me money from 10-years ago for welding I had done so the odds of getting paid this time were not good. That was when I said goodbye to everyone because I was mis-informed on the blade repair. If I had been told it was the pivot bushing, I would have never come up the winter road. Plus, the government was making the contractors plow the winter road open to the dirt. If it was the old way of plowing to leave 6"-8" of snow to be dragged for the snow base, then a temporary repair to the pivot bushing could have been made. I did not even stick around for a coffee and snack with the young kids in the camp and headed back to the Kingdom. I took more pictures as I drove along because I knew I had just wasted a lot of time and money to drive up the winter road to get pictures for my winter road book.

When I did arrive back in the Kingdom it was almost 1am and I made sure to take pictures of the pink crew cab on the security cameras on rewind to show the times I left and returned. The reason I take pictures of my security cameras on rewind. I had a customer that refused to pay me after I went out after regular business hours to weld on the drill rig. His staff did not tell him all the details of the simple breakage and when I sent my invoice to him, he spent 3-days yelling and screaming at me for over charging. I never really charged for call-out or after-hours welding rate.

(picture on cameras when I arrived back, Kingdom)

But the fellow accused me of overcharging because the drill rig was not broken until 2am in the morning according to his employee's time sheets. The reason why the employee's time sheets did not show the real time of the repair which would show how stupid they were and the big screw up they did. When I sent the fellow pictures of my security cameras with time of departure and return time. Then the pictures of welding at the drill rig to show the real damage. The fellow never said a word and sent a cheque for the full amount of my invoice 6-months later with no interest or bonus for the afterhours work. The next time the drill rig broke down and the fellow called me wanting me to perform magic. I gave him the telephone number for the welding shop in Thompson MB to travel 4-hours one way to weld the drill rig.

My new best friends did not make any money on the winter roads with the new government rates plus plowing wide and to the dirt. That was why the good contractor went home because he knew what it cost to build a winter road and run a business. The contractor's ex-employees that became my new best friends learned quickly about business. They never paid me or asked how much they owed me for traveling up the winter road that day. I am not an "asshole" and have served them meals in my house and they have drunk my beer too. I am English and will not forget because they will be paying for my time and expenses that day.

## Chapter 7
**Finally Paid**

(re-capping the timeline for new readers)

I could not deal with the Dumbass manager at the fuel company because he had no common sense. Xena and I had worked long and hard to make things run smoothly and kept our costs in line. The Dumbass manager was wasting money and misspending it faster than a person who won the 1-million-dollar lotto ticket at the 7-11 convenience store. Plus, the Dumbass manager liked yelling at me on the telephone which the 6'8" tattooed biker manager never did. I was now the Bride's Maid fixing the semi-trucks after hours and on weekends when the repair shops in Thompson MB were closed. This might have been not bad, but I was not charging the big rates the big repair shops charged for the afterhours work I was doing. In the 3-months of winter road repairs done in 2016, I only had invoices for $9400.00 which was not enough to cover the $2400.00 for 3-months of insurance to work on fuel semi-trucks. Also, there was the use of the pink crew cab for the truck drivers to use, the meals we cooked or bought the truck drivers, and the beer drank by the truck drivers. My Sesame Street Math was telling me there was no money in winter road repairs under the management of Dumbass. When the pup semi-trailer full of parts was taken out of the Kingdom it would be the last time. We had officially parted way with the fuel company after almost 12-years which we made friends with a lot of the drivers. The fuel company had gotten bad a paying my invoices and it was almost 6-months when they paid me for the little work I had done. But they had one invoice outstanding which was paid 2.5-years later on a Sunday morning at 7am when they called me with a broken truck. The new people working at the fuel company that replaced the Dumbass manager and his friends found out that the fuel company was not welcomed in WHO-ville or in the Kingdom. I told the new management that there was a problem when they were calling me at 7am on a Sunday morning because they had no other choices. The new management agreed and by 10am payment arrangements were made, and I did the repairs on the broke semi-truck. At the time of this writing in the year 2021, the fuel company that used to spend over $330,000.00 in a 3-month period for the winter road season from fuel, meals and repairs could not even use a telephone in WHO-ville. The covid 19 lock downs had everything closed and I did not want anything to do with the fuel company with the way I, was treated under the Dumbass manager. All my friends that worked at the fuel company were long gone and replaced by fly in truck drivers from the East coast. Any broken semi-truck or semi-trailer was now taken to Thompson MB for repairs or shipped the 1200km South to the head office of the fuel company. But all big companies today will use the fancy computer programs to show the company was making money. In 2012 a broke spring on the semi-truck was changed out for a $150.00 charge by the King of Obsolete. Plus, the semi-truck was back in rotation hauling fuel in 24-hours. Now the broken semi-truck sits in the trucker's parking in WHO-ville waiting for the Southern tow truck to arrive for the broken spring to be fixed in Thompson MB or Winnipeg MB. The broken spring repair had increased into the 1000s of dollars. I smile when I see these broke semi-trucks waiting and thankful, I no longer busting my ass for long hours to make a little bit of money. But I am thankful for the 12-

years of repairs to give me stories to write my books during the covid 19 lock downs.

(2019 the invoice was finally paid then we could do business again)

With the outstanding invoice finally paid the fuel company was sending broken fuel semi-trucks to the Kingdom for the little repairs. I could only repair certain things because there was no pup semi-trailer full of parts. The days of having lots of part to fix anything were long gone, I just did what I could. The problem I had with being famous on national TV for 15 seconds around the world. There were always the people that hate you when successful. My biggest haters were the people that had done nothing in their lives and think they are the greatest. I had an FM Radio in the office and could listen to the winter road semi-truckers talk on the FM Radio. I learned a long time ago that knowledge was power, and I just listened. Then when asked a question about something I knew the answer or location of the bad spots on the winter roads. The best one I got to enjoy was a group of semi-trucks arrived at WHO-ville. As they drove past the front gate of the Kingdom, one of the truck drivers made the comment that I was the King of "shit" not the King of Obsolete. I was very quiet as I listened to the truck drivers talk on the FM Radio. I got to learn that the fellow who called me the King of "shit" had a flat tire on the loaded semi-trailer. The group of semi-trucks went to the other repair businesses in WHO-ville only to find they were not open on a Saturday because they are never open on the weekends. I just listened the FM Radio as the group of semi-trucks chatted on the FM Radio what to do next. When they showed in the Kingdom, I was very polite and made it seem like I was interested in helping out these semi-trucks because I was famous. When the fellow showed me the blown tire on his semi-trailer, I told him I had a tire and everything to get him going on this fine Saturday afternoon. That made the truck driver very happy, and I could see that in his facial expressions. Then I told him that I am the King of "shit" and will not be working on his semi-trailer and "please" leave the Kingdom. Nobody said a thing as I walked away from them, and the truck drivers got back in their semi-trucks to leave the Kingdom. They never said anything bad about me on the FM Radio as the group of semi-trucks waited in WHO-ville at the trucker's parking lot for a replacement tire to arrive from Thompson MB in 6-hours.

The year 2019, I was the Bride's Maid numerous times with the other businesses being closed for the weekends. Then people would end up in my yard needing help. The semi-truck owner with the perfect hair that had always treated me like the Bride's Maid for the last 15-years showed up on a cold

Saturday morning. He brought along his new friends that were building the winter road to Tadoule MB. My new best friends that did winter road last year were broke financially thanks to the government and their cheaper winter road rates. Mr. Perfect Hair was so friendly and needed small trailer tires for his new best friends because the blew up tires on the so-called road. They needed to get up the winter road to start building the road and could not wait. I am not an asshole and let them have 2 of my spare tires for my tandem trailers I pull with the pink crew cab. I thought they would return my tires or be in contact with how to pay for them. It was a week later Mr. Perfect Hair was calling on a satellite phone from up the winter roads saying he was sending a fellow to the Kingdom to have a piece welded for the grader. It was Saturday so that was why I was getting the telephone call because the other businesses are closed. Mr. Perfect Hair told me the fellow would be there right away with the fellow traveling all night. He wanted me to weld it right away non-stop because the piece was for the grader which was very important with opening the winter road. I regret not telling Mr. Perfect Hair to take his business someplace else because in the 15-years I had not really made any money from this fellow. He was more of a pain-in the ass then anything plus hard to get paid from too. I guess I felt sorry for him, and I would help him out as a donation like all the other times.

I did not start any projects or do anything all day because the fellow that traveled all night with the pieces to be welded was to arrive anytime. To makes things worse my ex-fiancé the cop was working in WHO-ville making new friends because crime was out of control. My ex-fiancé would stop by the Kingdom to have coffee with me which I think was more of a tease. She was wearing the cop uniform and teased me by showing me a little bit of the "yellow" bra she was wearing. To me it looked grey being colour blind, but she told me I could find out what the true colour of her undies would be later on when she was done working as the cop. My ex-fiancé knew I went out with her as the mother of 4-daughters not the cop enforcing the laws of Canada. I did not really want to find out the colours of her granny panties or granny bra because I doubt, she would be wearing sexy undies like the cops in the pornographic films. My ex-fiancé had to leave the Kingdom because it being Saturday night crime was out of control in WHO-ville. I had wasted the whole day waiting for the fellow with the broken pieces to arrive for me to perform magic on welding them. At 10pm I needed my pain medication Vodka to calm me down because I had wasted the day for nothing. I should have just told Mr. Perfect Hair to take his business elsewhere because in the last 15-years he had wasted a lot of my time. My pain medication Vodka had closed my eyes at midnight only to be woken up by the telephone ringing. I answered the telephone thinking it might be my ex-fiancé wanting to come by the Kingdom to show me more of her "yellow" undies. But the telephone call was from the fellow traveling with the broken pieces saying he will be at the Kingdom Sunday morning. Then the telephone call was over with the fellow being out of range with the satellite phone he was using. Now this really "pissed" me off because nobody asked me to work Sunday or if I could work Sunday. People just excepted me to work while the other businesses in WHO-ville took the weekends off. Then come Monday morning, the customers I had done work for on the weekends are back at the other businesses. Once again, I am the Bride's Maid and will never be the Bride.

I told the fellow with the broken pieces not to come to the Kingdom before 10am Sunday morning because I had to be the King of Obsolete in the mornings. Every day I updated my website and chatted with people around the world. I can only do this first thing in the morning because that was the only time my expensive high-speed internet was fast. Living at the end of the world meant I was paying for high-speed internet that was not high speed but just faster than dial up speed. If I dare complain about the service, the internet company would cut my service or reduce my internet speed. I had read enough books and watched enough

YouTube videos to realize I was living in Stalin's Russia in Northern Manitoba. At 8am the fellow with the broken pieces arrived in the Kingdom and was telling me to hurry up and weld these pieces back together. The fellow had to get back up the winter roads because the grader was needed to open the winter road. Plus, if I hurry these pieces will not take long to weld. I was polite as I looked at the fellow, now I regret not tossing his "ass" out of my house so I could enjoy my relaxing Sunday morning. The pieces will take a bit to weld because the material was 1"-thick and bent when broken. The fellow then decided to drive in and out of the Kingdom to keep telling me to hurry up and hurry up with the welding. I worked non-stop to get the project done plus when 1"-steel was warm and being welded you cannot stop. As I welded away in my little shop, a semi-truck pulled in the Kingdom and up to the shop doors. The truck driver got out and was calling me his "friend" which I was not and never will be. I politely stop him as he was speaking and told him to get back in his semi-truck and leave out the back gate. The truck driver did not ask why because a year ago, Xena and I were leaving the Kingdom with a small cat on the trailer behind the pink crew cab. The truck driver had telephoned from the Dead Barn café saying he needed an air fitting for the semi-truck. I had lots of air fittings in stock in the Kingdom so I told the fellow to hurry up and we will wait for him. We gave up waiting for him because he never showed up and went to the other businesses in WHO-ville where the truck driver usually goes. I figured the truck driver walked out of the Dead Barn café to get in his semi-truck to drive to the Kingdom where Xena and I were waiting. As the truck driver crossed the street to walk to his parked semi-truck, the owner of the business that always fixed the semi-truck truck drove by. The business owner and the truck driver chatted then headed to the owner's business to fix the air fitting. Only problem was Xena and I waited an hour which costed money with the pink crew cab running along with the small cat. I could not charge the hour waiting because we were not at the winter drill roads plowing. Plus, everyone on the mineral claims asked where we were which we had to explain. That truck driver not showing up like he said he would be at the Kingdom costed my $500.00 plus the cost of the Vodka to take the pain away. The older I got the less of a nice guy I was becoming, and I have never done anything for that trucker driver ever since.

With the truck driver gone, I went back to welding and welding some more to finish up the broken pieces for the grader. The fellow returned at 9pm at night when I was just finishing the magic I had to perform. The fellow then wanted other things to make the project a success with a shopping list as if he was at the parts store in Winnipeg MB. I just wanted the day to end so I could enjoy my pain medication Vodka because I was in pain. I write all the extras down and the fellow finally left at 10pm at night Sunday night. To my understanding the fellow was going to drive all night back up the winter roads to be there in the morning. Then the road crew could put the welded piece back on the grade and head to Tadoule MB. My pain medication Vodka closed my eye quickly that night and I never opened any emails from my ex-fiancé to see what colour of undies she was wearing under the cop uniform. In the morning I got off to a slow start with my body being sore from non-stop welding on 1"-steel and the Vodka hurting my head for some reason. I did all my paperwork on this Monday morning and emailed off my invoices for the last week's work. By 10am I had enough coffee to drink to wake up and feel like I am going to make it through a Monday. It was a steady day in the Kingdom with little jobs here and there, but I was glad when the day was over. I enjoyed my pain medication Vodka and the sexy pictures my ex-fiancé had emailed me of her in the Big Bird "yellow" undies that she was wearing under the cop uniform. But she was out making new friends back in Grief Rapids and did not reply to my emails.

It was Tuesday at noon when I came out of the little shop to walk up to the house for lunch. When the fellow I had welded the pieces for, pulled up to me as I stood there. I had figured he had driven up the winter roads and dropped off the welded pieces and now returned with more to be welded. But I was so wrong because he went everywhere but back up the winter roads. The welded pieces were still in the back of the truck where I had put them late Sunday night. The fellow now wanted more items from my inventory which I told him "no" and walked away. I think the fellow had been partying with the local ladies for the last 2-days which pissed me off. I had wasted my Sunday working and rushing for nothing only for him to go partying. Now I regret sending my invoice off to be paid on Monday because I never really charged for after hours or weekend rates. Now I was pissed, and the invoice would be doubled for what I had done and being told to hurry up. Being told to hurry up will get me so pissed off because I had to rush for their lack of organization. It was 3-months later I was telephoning Mr. Perfect Hair to find out where my money was for the invoice I sent. Mr. Perfect Hair had 101 excuses why he had not mailed me payment which included his dog ate his cheque book. I was not impressed and was polite in saying goodbye on the telephone. Then a month later the gay guy running the Dead Barn café called me personally on a Sunday morning. As I listened on my cordless phone, the gay guy tells me that he had phoned all the repairs shops in WHO-ville and they are not around to fix this broken semi-truck. The most insulting part to me was when the gay guy told me that I was the "last" to be called and really hoped I could help out. I was just smiling when the gay guy handed the telephone to the truck driver. The truck driver was all polite and desperate in hoping I would fix the semi-truck because all the other businesses were not open or around. I was polite when I told the truck driver that I am not the Bride's Maid, and his boss still has not paid my invoice from 4-months ago. I then said goodbye and was smiling as I poured a nice glass of my new victory drink called Vodka. When Xena picked up the mail 4-days later at the WHO-ville post office. There was cheque written and dated on that Sunday when I told the truck driver that I was owed money and no repairs will take place. I was very surprised to get any money from Mr. Perfect Hair and I should have charged 4-times as much on that invoice for the non-stop work and the stress I received. But I did get paid which was the main thing because a lot of companies do not pay these days.

## Chapter 8
**Washed & Waxed**


On January 06, 2019, I got a telephone call while I was working in the little shop. I answered the call on my cordless phone because it was my friend Bob from Kinoosao SK. He told me on the telephone that he took his 2006 Ford F150 for a swim in reindeer lake. I told him that was not good because he must have found the only weak spot in the ice on the lake. Bob told me he did, and they were able to get out of the Ford as it slowly sunk beneath the ice. He and his daughter with her young son were able to make a fire on shore with the toothpick trees and use the satellite phone to call back to Kinoosao for help.

The fire slowly dried out their clothes because they were wet from the waist down. But it was still cold and hard to keep the fire going till the ski-doos arrived from Kinoosao. Bob told me that the 20-mile ski-doo ride back to Kinoosao was the coldest he had ever been, but he was alive. His daughter and grandson were cold too riding on the ski-doos. The problem Bob had was the insurance company will cover the Ford truck because he was driving to work.

(last picture of the Ford truck before going under)

Bob traveled up and down reindeer lake every Sunday for his job at the South end of the reindeer lake. In the summer he traveled by boat and when there was not much snow on the ice on reindeer lake, he could drive his Ford truck. All other times he had to drive his ski-doo for the one week at work then one week at home in Kinoosao. Bob had done this for years and it was only 3-4-hours traveling one way and he could always hunt or fish on the trip. The insurance company wanted a full assessment of the Ford truck in the lake, and he called me to help. I told Bob I would call the insurance company for him to get things happening for him to get money to get another vehicle.

When I called the insurance company that had heard of me from my 15 seconds of fame on the TV show Ice Road Truckers. The insurance company was willing to cut a deal that Bob got his insurance money to buy another vehicle and I got the Ford truck in the frozen lake. Since I had spent so much money on lawyers over the years which I could have went to law school myself. I drew up a fancy letter that made everyone happy and the insurance company paid out Bob's insurance claim. Plus, the people of Kinoosao got employment and I got the Ford truck that was Washed and Waxed in reindeer lake. Bob was so happy this happened, and he could not believe it. I was happy too because I get film, pictures and the story to market. Bob got his insurance money and bought a nice SUV vehicle which would be better for traveling with his grandson then a Ford truck. All I had to do was wait for the ice to thicken up to support the salvage operation of the Ford truck in the frozen lake. I let Bob handle all this because the locals have salvaged lots of sunk trucks in reindeer lake. Bob kept me posted on the salvage operation that happened around the first of March 2019. They had to wait that long to the ice to thicken up and everyone to join in on the fun project. Bob sent me pictures of the Ford truck sitting back up on the ice of reindeer lake then I could make plans.

The scrap guy and his ladies had been hauling scrap out of WHO-ville and the scrap guy agreed to join me on this adventure. Xena had to stay and run the business plus it was only a little day trip to reindeer lake and back. The day trip was based on the scrap guy and his ladies because he had 2-lady truck drivers which drove back and forth to Winnipeg MB loaded with scrap metal for recycling. The scrap guy timed it on March 26, 2019, that the ladies will be headed South loaded with scrap and that would give us time for a quick drive on the frozen reindeer lake. The scrap guy spent that Friday getting both ladies loaded with scrap, so they were gone that night. I was getting everything loaded up with the pink crew cab and Thor the plow truck for this adventure. But every time I went to the cardlock in WHO-ville to get fuel of the adventure there was a lodge owner blocking all the pumps to fill fuel barrels on the deck of his semi-trailer. This lodge owner was an asshole, and I would not waste my time even talking to him because we did not hit it off very well when he first bought a lodge on reindeer lake. I just drove up to the cardlock every hour to see if the asshole was done filling his fuel barrels or moved his semi-truck enough that other customers could use the other 2-fuel pumps. The asshole blocked off the fuel pumps at the cardlock for 4-hours which pissed off a lot of people in WHO-ville but the lodge owner was an asshole and did not care. When I was finally done with getting, the equipment ready and fueled up. The scrap guy was done loading the 2-ladies to head South. We all cooked a big meal in the Kingdom so the ladies would have food for their trip South and we would have food for out on reindeer lake. The ladies left at 9pm for the long slow trip over the so-called road to Thompson MB. The scrap guy and I could barely stay awake at 11pm so it was bedtime for us. If there were no problems with the ladies heading to Thompson MB, then we could officially leave at 6am in the morning for reindeer lake. Once the ladies were near or close to Thompson MB, if they had any problems there were people around to help them. But getting to Thompson MB meant that we would have to head over the so-called road to fix or repair what broke on the semi-trucks. The ladies were pulling high sided Super B trailers loaded with scrap metal and only had to worry about the straps holding the plastic mesh on top of the load down. One lady was driving a Peterbilt with a big Caterpillar motor while the other lady was driving a Kenworth with a big Detroit motor. All these ladies talked about at meals time whose truck was better and whose had more horsepower. If you closed your and imagine the ladies were talking with deep voices you would swear, they were men. But the scrap guy was happy they were gone with no troubles when we woke up at 5am to find out if we were going to reindeer lake today.

(the 2-car parade on the Kinoosao Rally Road)

With all messages good from both ladies then we could leave for reindeer lake. Before we left the Kingdom, I sent a message by Facebook to Kinoosao that we would be arriving. I drove the pink crew cab pulling the high deck tandem trailer with the supplies on the deck. The scrap guy drove the plow truck named Thor because he had driven it all winter plowing snow to find the scrap he was hauling. Thor was pulling the low deck tandem trailer which had the TD-6 on the deck. The only problem we had; I took the snowplow off the front of Thor because we thought we did not need it on this trip. The snowplow was needed because the weight of the snowplow gave Thor decent ride on the front. But no plow meant the scrap guy had a rough ride in the cab and felt every little bump in the road on his back. The Kinoosao Rally Road was excellent to drive on because it had melted then frozen. The 100km trip over the rally road only took 3.5-hours of traveling with no breakage. When we arrived in Kinoosao it was a nice sunny day which was going to be good for film and pictures of this fun adventure. We parked Thor and unload the TD-6 cat then got everything ready to go with the pink crew cab. Bob's son showed up at the perfect time to get in the pink crew cab to be our guide on reindeer lake. I am driving the TD-6 and will use the vee plow to plow a trail for the pink crew cab to follow along behind me. The scrap guy will drive the pink crew cab with Bob's son riding along. The trick to reindeer lake was the snow conditions because there were 4-styles of snow conditions going to where the Ford truck was. One thing I learned on reindeer lake over the 22 years of having fun on it was not to waste time plowing snow. Just plow enough for the pink crew cab to follow plus plow fast. Speed when plowing makes a big difference on busting through the snow drifts. We made good time and I plowed beside the asshole lodge owner's trail he had made with his $150,000.00 in fancy snowcats to pull sleds with a little bit of product to his lodge. The asshole lodge owner was at the cardlock filling fuel barrels then arrived back in Kinoosao that evening. Now this morning he headed to his lodge with his fancy snowcats. The lodge owner was such an asshole that he could make a swing passed a stuck vehicle on reindeer lake so the people could at least attempt to get it out.

(plowing our ice road on reindeer lake)

As I plowed along, I made my ice road go right beside the stuck vehicle so it could be shoveled out of the snowbank and driven to Kinoosao. If the keys were in the vehicle, we would have pulled it out and on to the new ice road I was plowing for the owners, but no keys and it was locked. Bob's son had sent a message to the owners on Facebook saying that I would be plowing right by the vehicle like I had done in the past. Even the scrap guy could not get over how much of an asshole the lodge owner was but not making his trail close to help out the stuck vehicle. Oh well, was all we said because the lodge owner must have lots of guests at his lodge to afford all these expensive fun toys.

(the Washed and Waxed Ford truck being loaded)

I drove the TD-6 non-stop with as much speed as I could for the next 5 hours to get where the Ford truck was sitting on top of the ice on reindeer lake. We arrived and do not wasted any time loading the Ford truck on to the high deck tandem trailer then headed back to Kinoosao. Going back was easy because the vee plow on the TD-6 was just dressing up the ice road we had just plowed. The TD-6 was in 5th gear and flat out for speed with the pink crew cab following along.

(heading back over the new ice road as the sun set)

The trip across reindeer lake brought back memories for the scrap guy. When he was a young truck driver, he drove across the ice to Brochet MB to deliver freight. The last official ice road across reindeer lake to Brochet MB was 22 years ago in 1997 which only seemed like yesterday. On the last 5-mile stretch into Kinoosa, the lodge owner was returning from his lodge with his fancy equipment.

The track machines were slow moving dragging the sleds and traveling on top of the snow on the ice of reindeer lake. But we had an ice road freshly plowed which we were traveling fast on. When we caught up to the lodge owner, he would not even look at us or wave to us as we were side by side only 50-feet apart. Once passed the slow-moving lodge owner we made good time on our new ice road. The stuck vehicle was gone from where it was stuck, and the tracks appear that they were able to drive the vehicle on our ice road to Kinoosao.

Once back in Kinoosao, we loaded up the TD-6 cat on to the low deck trailer pulled Thor and dropped off Bob's son. We thanked him for guiding us on reindeer lake which gave him something to do. The scrap guy and I were gone out of Kinoosao as the lodge owner arrived with his slow-moving fancy equipment. We had just plowed a 20-mile road down the lake in 5-hours and return in 3.5-hours. If the lodge owner was not such an asshole, we could have plowed an ice road to his lodge and back in ½ the time it took to drive the fancy slow equipment that hauled really nothing. The drive back to the Kingdom was boring and when we arrived the scrap guy was worried about his ladies. When he got internet and could check on the 2-scrap semi-trucks both were unloaded and heading back to WHO-ville for another load. Now the scrap guy could not relax the next day to recover from the fun day or driving

Thor over the Kinoosao Rally Road. He had to get the scrap metal ready for the ladies who will be back the next day. The Ford truck was salvageable, and I had the vehicle up and running to be sold as is where is. A little water never hurt anything if removed correctly.

## Chapter 9
**Meet Thor**


A Kingdom Follower wanted me to buy a plow truck for the Kingdom which I did not think was a good idea. But 3-years later I bought the plow truck in December 2018 which became known as Thor. The scrap guy and his ladies picked up the truck on December 24, 2018 and drove Thor to his shop. Thor spent Xmas in the warm shop getting thawed out because the scrap guy and ladies were going to paint Thor to match the Black Fleet in the Kingdom. I told the scrap guy to get Rust-o-Leum paint with brushes and paint rollers to splash the paint on Thor. Plus use the correct amount of Vodka to make the paint stick but the scrap guy lives in the South. Splashing paint on a vehicle with a paint brush and roller was not what the Southern sociality accepts. But in the Great White North splashing the paint on nice and thick with lots of runs made the paint job and vehicle look good. The scrap guy and his ladies used masking tape and paper to cover up the chrome plus all other items that did not needed to be painted black. For us splashing the paint on meant that the chrome and everything else got painted over too. That was why the correct amount of Vodka was needed to loosen up your body, so the paint flowed correctly when splashed on. I had figured only 4-hours to paint Thor and then 2-days for the thick splashed on paint to dry. The scrap guy was 3-days with masking and taping, cleaning and then spraying the black paint on then watching it dry. Plus, the scrap guy even had stick-on-decals to add the King of Obsolete and Thor to the side of the plow truck. I had never heard of getting decals made up because I just drank the correct amount of Vodka then painted the name on anything I owned free hand. Too much Vodka meant the letters were not that straight, but the paint was far from good but good from a far. After a week in the scrap guy's shop, Thor was done and the Xmas holidays over. Then the scrap guy and his ladies headed back North to haul more scrap from WHO-ville. The scrap guy needed the plow truck for find his scrap metal that got buried in all the snow that arrived over the Xmas holidays.

I never got to drive Thor because the scrap guy was having fun driving around plowing snow. I was very impressed at how much Thor could plow and I was glad I called the truck Thor. Just like in the mythical character, Thor smashes through the snowbank like the big hammer Thor carried. But I did get to work on Thor between the plowing because Thor needed to be upgraded. Thor was a USA Air Force 1983 IH Paystar 5000 4x4 plow truck spec'd to plow the runways at the air force bases. Thor was to ensure the Nuclear Bombers could be airborne on a moment's notice during the cold war. Now Thor was at the end of the world in the Great White North where speed plowing a long smooth runway was long gone. Thor was now going to bounce off every rock that was in the ground plus bounce over the winter roads to make a living. When Thor was at the scrap guy's shop in the South over the Xmas holidays. The scrap guy made improvements to the plow controls to be operated by one person in the cab of Thor. The USA Air Force had the truck spec'd for 2-people to be in the cab at all times as the safety buddy system. The USA Air Force had 1-person driving the truck while the passenger of the truck was known as the "wing man" controlling all plow functions. This worked good but in Northern Canada the odds of having a "wing man" are very slim unless they are your offspring. I never thought nothing of the new controls the scrap guy had set up in Thor because he was doing all the driving and plowing with Thor. Even when we went to reindeer lake to pick up the Ford truck that was Washed & Waxed in the frozen lake. The scrap guy drove Thor there and back while I drove the pink crew cab listening to the same Heavy Metal Music CD that had been stuck in the CD player for the last year.

(Thor 1983 IH Paystar 5000 USA Air Force)

Finally, the scrap guy and his ladies were done the scrap metal in WHO-ville and headed South. We said goodbye and they would be back with hauling my new purchases from the South. Then we got the usual big snowstorm in April 2019, and I had to drive Thor the plow truck for the first time. It was a disaster because I could not operate the plow controls. The scrap guy was left-handed and set the control switches up for a left-handed person to operate. I am right-handed and could not get the plow controls set to my liking. I made the mistake of asking Xena to help and see what she thought of the plow controls. Xena drove Thor and operated the plow controls with no problems because she was left-handed too. It was decided that I should not be changing the plow controls for a right-handed person to use because the truck will be driven by Xena as I get older. The best way to describe driving and operating Thor the plow truck was to pretend to be the drummer Nicko McBrain for the English band Iron Maiden who was very busy when playing the song Number of the Beast. Plus, the 250 cummins motor in Thor put out a lot of heat even when the motor was idling. Then the sweat would be dripping down your forehead as you did any snow plowing in the Kingdom. The cummins motor was the total opposite then the 8V71 detroit that put out no heat unless screaming for mercy with fresh oil added daily. The 250 cummins was an inline 6 cylinder that used no oil or dripped oil and put out way too much heat.

Throughout the summer of 2019, Thor got used to pull the tandem trailers around when the loads were too big for the pink crew cab. Plus, sometimes we just used Thor to pull the trailer for photo opportunities. Any time I posted pictures of Thor on my website or on Facebook there was always lots of good reviews. Also, a lot of people could not believe that a USA Air Force plow truck was in the

Kingdom at the end of the world. But Thor was proving me wrong because I thought the truck had no place in the Kingdom being a Southern plow truck. That was why it took 3-years for me to purchase Thor and if the fellow did not keep calling me and telling me this was the truck I needed. Then I finally bought Thor and never looked back with the truck being very handy in the Kingdom. When the snows came in October 2019, Thor was being used to keep the Kingdom clear of snow. I slowly learned how to operate the left-handed plow controls as I learned how useful Thor was by being so fast at plowing snow. The true test for Thor came in December 2019 with the fish haul from Kinoosao SK. Someone decided that after 30-year of no winter fishing they were going to fish reindeer lake. The idea had to be the government because it was dumbest idea I had ever heard of in the last couple of weeks. I follow along on the government website for tenders and as the smart people in government retired, the young upper educated people were taking over. The tender website became a form of entertainment for me every morning as I enjoy my morning coffee in the Kingdom. The tenders that were being offered were funny then the bid amounts were even more funny with very stupid prices. Now I knew the winter fishing on reindeer lake was going to be a failure because the infrastructure for winter fishing was gone. The fishermen got rid of the bombardier that had a woodstove to keep them warm while pulling the nets out on ice. The fishermen were buying the fancy fast ski-doos for the same price as a good used bombardier. But a ski-doo offered no warmth and only carried 2-people. Oh well the world had changed big time in the 30-years since they last winter fished reindeer lake.

I did not think I was going to get involved with the fish hauling except for the repairs to the semi-trucks hauling the fish from Kinoosao. It was at 2pm on December 06, 2019, when the telephone rang with an important call. The head of the big trucking company in Thompson MB was calling to ask me to handle it because his world fell apart. The fuel tanks at the big trucking company in Thompson MB got a bad batch of diesel fuel delivered from the South. It was Southern diesel fuel which can be used until the temperatures dropped to being really cold. That was what had happened with extreme cold weather coming to Northern Manitoba. Now the 200-semi-truck and 200-diesel powered refrigeration units were all quitting everywhere in Northern Manitoba. I was all smiles because I knew what had happened with the diesel fuel. Some new young person hired by the big trucking company was going to save the company big money by purchasing diesel fuel at 4-cents cheaper being Southern fuel. Then ship it North to save a lot of money pre-day with everything that used diesel fuel. This was great plan and if anyone in the head office had any common sense or knew anything about trucking would have stop the money saving idea before it got started. Now everything in the North had the cheap Southern diesel being used and the cold weather had not hit Northern Manitoba until December 05, 2019. The overnight temperature went down to -43f which stopped any with the South diesel fuel from flowing because it became a syrup not a liquid form. The head of the big trucking company just told me to handle it which meant break all the rules to get it done because there was a lot of money involved. The biggest concern was the weekly beer truck heading to WHO-ville was broke down by Grief Rapids. It is not the cost of $40,000.00 in beer being stole, it was the damage and health problems that $40,000.00 in beer will cause. The thieves will share the beer and people will drink too much then start fighting. When they fight, people get hurt and need to be taken to the hospital. If they got hurt really bad, then a medivac airplane flies from Winnipeg MB to pick up the people that are really hurt then fly back to Winnipeg MB. We always figured that $40,000.00 in stolen beer would cost be an easy $600,000.00 which would affect the social system of the North. With the cops, medical and the medivac flights plus it could cost a few people their lives.

I did not have the Screaming Ford plugged in to warm up the 8V71 detroit motor because it was the off season for us with work. I had to wait a couple of hours for the motor to warm up which I also added the diesel fired heater to blow heat under the front of the Screaming Ford. It was 8pm when I was able to leave the Kingdom in the Screaming Ford. The plan was simple with pulling the broken semi-trucks out from under the van semi-trailers of freight. The big trucking company did not care about the broken semi-trucks because they had to be hauled South to a warm shop to be thawed out. The main concern was the van semi-trailers and the diesel-powered refrigeration units. It maybe -40f but the refrigeration units are heating units too which keep everything inside the van semi-trailers at the correct temperature. When I arrived at the beer truck on the side of the road. The first thing, I did was put diesel fuel conditioner in the fuel tank for the refrigeration unit. Then I made the unit run fast and hard to get the diesel fuel to flow to mix in the fuel conditioner. These diesels powered refrigeration units are a pain in the "ass" because they are mounted high up on the front of the van semi-trailer and the fuel tank was mount down low under the van semi-trailer. If the unit quit, it was very hard to get the fuel to come back up almost 15-feet of fuel lines to the diesel motor. To keep the diesel motors to stay running was 100% luck on most days now add extreme cold and bad fuel. But it was my lucky day with keeping the refrigeration unit running. Once I was happy that it would stay running, I now dragged the broken semi-truck out from under the van semi-trailer. The Screaming Ford had the 30,000lbs Wicked Winch that just dragged anything out of the way. A new style semi-truck with the park brakes on just slid out from under the van semi-trailer no problem.

Once hooked up to the van semi-trailer with the beer, I headed back towards WHO-ville but I now had weight on the drive wheels of the Screaming Ford. The beer truck was the last of 3-semi-trucks heading to WHO-ville that quit on the so-called road. I had stopped at the other broken semi-trucks to put diesel fuel conditioner in the diesel tanks of the refrigeration units as I headed to the beer truck. The items inside these van semi-trailers were not as important as the beer. If the refrigeration unit quit and the insides of the van semi-trailer cooled off, then it would not be as much of a problem. The beer was the most important cargo on any of the 3-van semi-trailers that day. I pulled in front of the broken semi-truck and since the Screaming Ford was hooked to the loaded beer semi-trailer, I would have traction to pull the broken semi-truck out from under the van semi-trailer. This was a lot easier to do then winching the broken semi-truck out from under the van semi-trailer. With room to hook up to the van semi-trailer when I came back, I now drove the Screaming Ford on to the next broken semi-truck to do the same thing with pulling it out from underneath. I learned the older I got; it was best to work smarter not harder in these extreme cold temperatures. Back in the Kingdom, I dopped off the beer semi-trailer and headed back down the so-called road to pick up the next van semi-trailer. The Screaming Ford worked excellent in the cold temperatures which was good because if the truck had broken down then I would freeze waiting for Xena to come and rescue me in the pink crew cab. It was 3am when I had all 3-van semi-trailers in the Kingdom with the Screaming Ford hooked back up to the beer semi-trailer. I left the Screaming Ford run all night which was music to my ears but the diesel motor sounds from the refrigeration units was a sound I could never get used to. When I poured my first glass of my pain medication Vodka, my ex-fiancé telephoned the Kingdom at 3:22am because she was still being the cop. She was glad that I had all the van semi-trailers off the so-called road because if anything got stolen out of the van semi-trailers the paperwork would be unreal for the cops. Now in the eyes of my ex-fiancé I was a hero for risking it all with the Screaming Ford to keep the beer from falling into the hands of the career criminals. My ex-fiancé cannot really talk to me on the telephone at the cop shop wearing her cop uniform with her cop co-workers sitting around listening to her talk. But she was teasing me by telling what she was going to do to me in the bedroom later this week. She was talking on the telephone as the cop co-workers listened that she was going handcuff me and then use the taser on me too. Oh my, was all I could reply because I knew the taser hurt because I still had the mark on my "ass" when she zapped me one night when the booze beverages tasted too good. I said goodbye to my ex-fiancé before she really got carried away on saying bad things on the telephone. Now my pain medication Vodka closed my eyes because the extreme cold weather had worn me out at my age.

In the morning I was having my morning coffee to wake up to see if I was going to survive after the long cold night. The telephone rang which I answered it to find a drunk lady trying to talk sober. She was calling wanting beer that was in the van semi-trailer to keep the party going. She promised to pay for the beer when the hotel vendor opened at 10am but needed the beer now. She even promised to do bad things to me when she came to pick up the beer in the Kingdom. I politely told her that the beer semi-trailer was not in the Kingdom, and it was in Grief Rapids. Now the drunk lady called me a liar because she knew the beer truck broke down and I had all beer. Now she was coming over to get some beer for the party. I had to think fast because that was the last thing, I wanted was drunk people in the Kingdom who would not be taking no for an answer. I told the drunk lady on the telephone that my ex-fiancé, the cop had spent the night in the Kingdom. The cop would be very upset with her coming over to do bad things to me for beer. Then the drunk lady said goodbye and hung up the telephone. The Kingdom was the perfect place to have the beer semi-trailer parked with 16-cameras and 5-guard dogs with lots of yard lights and gates. Now I could go back to enjoying my morning coffee after 10-minutes of drama. When it was time to go outside with the temperature at -38c, I "popped" the tire chains on the Screaming Ford to make deliveries around WHO-ville. I had 2-van semi-trailers to deliver with the beer being first. Once the 2-van semi-trailers were delivered, I hooked on to the 3rd van semi-trailer to deliver to Kinoosao SK. I was told that the community had a brand-new bouncy backhoe which all the snow would had been done at the fish plant. I knew this would be all lies like my marriage and that was why I had left the tire chains on the Screaming Ford.

The Kinoosao Rally Road had been freshly plowed by the department of highways which was a lame-ass job. The grader operator was a young kid that drove the new grader by the speedometer not by the grader blade cutting the snow off the road. The Screaming Ford had the triple tire chains on, and I could feel the truck trying to get tractions on the little hills close to Kinoosao. The young kid was watching the speedometer on the new style grader and had lifted the blade up from cutting the snowpack of the road base. I had graded this road for 2-years with an old Champion grader as part of my "real job". The hills and curves had to be cut down for traction and the flat straight stretches of the road were not really worried about. But the government trying to save money was making the Kinoosao Rally Road worse with new style equipment. At km90 hill which was a curve and hill combined, the Screaming Ford was digging and fighting for traction on the back wheels that were all chained up. That was when I knew there was no way the loaded fish semi-truck would be able to make it out of Kinoosao fully loaded. But I was also all smiles because the government doing a terrible job grading the road meant I will be getting the plowing and towing of the load fish semi-truck. The last 10kms to Kinoosao was terrible and the Screaming Ford was fighting all the way to get tractions with the tire chains on the rear wheels. I arrived in Kinoosao to find the snow had not been plowed but I knew that. I had been coming here for over 20-years and snow plowing in the community was not high priority. I knew I could not drive to the fish plant on the South side of the community, so I turned the Screaming Ford around at the first street by the Kinoosao Rally Road. Then I back the van semi-trailer all the way through town and dropped it by the fish plant. The snow was not done, and nobody really cared but they had the brand-new bouncy backhoe with forks that could carry the totes full of fish to the van semi-trailer where I had parked it. I serviced the refrigeration unit to make sure it would stay running in the cold overnight temperatures of -42f. After a quick call to Xena to say I was heading back to the Kingdom from Kinoosao, I headed home. The big hill just outside of Kinoosao was graded very lame ass with lots of snow packed left on the road. The Screaming Ford just barely made it up the big hill spinning the rear wheels all the way trying to get traction. I was all smiles again because the government owned grader did a terrible job which will be money in my pocket when the first fish semi-truck tries to climb the big hill out of Kinoosao.

After the big hill out of Kinoosao on the Kinoosao Rally Road there were 4 more hills that were plowed the same way with leaving lots of snow packed to maintain speed in the new style grader. The Screaming Ford had traction problems on all these slightly small hills which made me smile. I was making good time until I got to the start of the winter road. When I went to Kinoosao there were 2-Chevy contractor style trucks parked at the start of the road. The winter road was not plowed because it was only the beginning of December. These contractor trucks were hunters from Flin Flon MB that came up to shoot a caribou or a moose which ever came first. Now on my return trip, the hunters were back with their ski-doos and the one truck would not start. They were trying to boost it with the one truck that was running which was not working very well. I pulled the Screaming Ford alongside because the batteries are on the driver's side of the truck. These hunters recognized me from my 15 seconds of fame on national TV on the Ice Road Truckers show. We chatted as the booster cables from the Screaming Ford to the non-running truck let power transfer to add life to the dead batteries. The hunters had left work in Flin Flon to drive and arrive in WHO-ville at 1am in the morning. The cardlock fuel station would not let them get any fuel because the trigger on the fuel nozzle would not click in with the extreme temperature we were having. I then told the hunters that the card lock owner was cheap and only bought cheap fuel nozzles. If they had shoved a big screwdriver into the plunger on the nozzle then fuel would have come out. The hunters just looked at me in shock because they could not get fuel and had to sleep in their trucks. In the morning at 7am, they went to the gas station in WHO-ville but the diesel pump would not pump fuel because it was too cold. They had spent 2-hours as the pump slowly gave a little trickle of fuel. The fellow who owned the gas station told them the filters needed changing on the diesel pump which he had on the table by the window. I then told the hunters that those filters had been sitting on the table by the window for 2-years. The gas station owner does not really care about changing them or having repeat customers. I then welcomed the hunters to WHO-ville where there was no customer service. Now the hunters were not too impressed because had wasted a lot of time that should not have been wasted. Plus, they ski-dooed up the winter roads and seen nothing for animal tracks. To really upset the hunters even more, I told them I last time I had seen a moose in 2014 because locals had been shooting anything that moves because that was their given right to hunt any time. The caribou had not been down the winter roads in also 4-years because of the forest fires burnt everything they eat. The caribou goes where the food was for them to eat which did not impress the hunters at all.

With enough chatting and the batteries in the non-running Chevy charged up, the one hunter tried to start the motor. It would not start only crank over with the bad fuel in it from the gas station. I reminded the hunters if the diesel pump at the gas station was not pumping very fast in the cold it was not good winter fuel. As the one hunter cranked the motor over, I gave the motor a "sniff of ether" starting fluid which should have excited the motor or blown it up but there was nothing. I told the hunters they could follow me back to the Kingdom and use my car trailer to load up this non-running Chevy. The hunters just looked at me and were unsure what to do. I then offered to tow the truck back to the Kingdom behind the Screaming Ford with stopping every 15-minutes to change out the frozen driver. They agreed to that offer because 15-minutes in a non-running vehicle was no different than riding a ski-doo at -40f. I had made this offer because the hunters were smart guys and mechanical inclined which made towing easy. I cannot see the non-running Chevy behind the Screaming Ford in the dark. So, I set my magnetic re-chargeable flashlights on the hood. Now I could see the vehicle plus the person steering had some sort of lights to see the Screaming Ford. These re-chargeable flashlights worked great and last a long time in the cold weather. The 1-hour drive from the start of the winter road to the Kingdom was done in 1.5-hours because these hunters knew how to steer a vehicle being towed. Once in the Kingdom we pushed the front of the non-running Chevy truck just inside the little shop doors like all other vehicles before. As the hunters tarped in the vehicle, I put more wood in the wood stove to heat up the little shop. Then I got my diesel fire heater on wheels to blow heat under the front of the vehicle to warm it up. It only took 2-hours, and the non-running Chevy was running again. I had put lots of fuel conditioner in the fuel tank and gave the hunters fuel conditioner for the trip home. They left the Kingdom at 11pm to drive straight through to Flin Flon MB. At 10am in the morning they called me on the telephone to say they made it with no problems plus thanked me again. After they had left, my pain medication Vodka was calling my name because it was a long night then a long day for me.

With the van semi-trailer in Kinoosao, the fishermen were not delivering the fish they had caught to the fish plant. The reason was the ice was not thick enough to support the weight of vehicles driven on the ice. The fishermen were doing everything by ski-doo. Nobody owned a bombardier like they had used 30-years ago when they winter fished. Now the big trucking company ask me to deliver diesel fuel to the van semi-trailer in Kinoosao because the fuel tank only lasted 3-days. The van semi-trailer should have been filled with totes of fish in 2-days. Then the loaded van semi-trailer would be switched out for an empty one to be filled with totes of fish. Now I got to drive to Kinoosao and fill up the diesel fuel tank on the van semi-trailer that kept the refrigeration unit running. It was a nice drive to Kinoosao and back in the pink crew cab for only 15 minutes of work in the -37c daytime temperature. Plus, I checked over the diesel motor to make sure everything was ok in the extreme cold temperatures. The locals loading the totes of fish figured the van semi-trailer will be ready the next day to be shipped South. The fish from reindeer lake will be in downtown Chicago in less than 4-days where they are cooked in a fancy café. These fish had been going South since the early 1940s when fishing on reindeer lake was big business. The drive back to the

Kingdom was boring with not meeting any traffic on the Kinoosao Rally Road. This was not good in case the pink crew cab broke down. Up in the Great White North everything was based on survival. Back in the Kingdom I call the truck driver Johnny in Grief Rapids who usually hauls the van semi-trailer of fish out of Kinoosao. I touched base with Johnny on the road condition and the fact that he will not be able to get up the hills on the Kinoosao Rally Road the way they are plowed. Johnny agreed and we decided it would be best if I had the plow truck Thor ready to come and rescue him. Johnny will also stop by the Kingdom on the way to Kinoosao to borrow my satellite phone so he can call me while stuck on the big hill. Johnny having my satellite phone will save him from having to walk the 4kms back to Kinoosao to use a telephone to call me. I did not enjoy my pain medication Vodka too much that night because I knew the next day was going to be a long day getting Johnny up the big hill by Kinoosao.

Johnny stopped by the Kingdom on his way to Kinoosao to borrow my satellite phone. Johnny and I have been up and down the Kinoosao Rally Road lots with the fish haul with him being stuck in the sand at Kinoosao or broken down. Now this will be the first-time having fun in the winter at -37c for the winter fishing. Johnny figured it would 3pm when he would know if he did not make the big hill coming out of Kinoosao. I told him I would have

Thor the plow truck running and ready to come and rescue him. That made Johnny happy as he left the Kingdom to drive to Kinoosao. Right at 3pm, Johnny called to say he did not make the big hill in fact he did not even make it up the hill to the steep part. I told Johnny I was on my way because I was waiting for his call. This was now the official first trip for Thor over the snow-covered roads which will be his retirement job. Plus, this was my first time actually driving the truck as a plow truck in the winter. Since I plowed the Kinoosao road for 2-years, I knew which places to plow and where not to plow. The first hill and curve that I had to plow was going down for me because coming back from Kinoosao it would be uphill for the fish truck. I put the expensive tire chains on the back of Thor for the first time and made sure they were tight. Then I had to learn how to plow a hill with rocks with an airport plow truck. It was so cold the hydraulics took forever to do anything but the more I used them the better they got for speed. Also, an airport plow truck cannot put pressure down on the snowplow blades, so I had to learn how to make them cut the snowpack down. It did not take me long to figure out the expensive tire chains cut the snow packed road plus different angles on the front snowplow. It was taking about 6-8-passes to cut down the hills that had over 8" of snow packed left by the young kid driving the grader for the highways department. But the young kid had all the flat straight parts of the Kinoosao Rally Road cut right down. This was the total opposite to how the Kinoosao Rally Road was to be plowed.

I arrived in Kinoosao in 4-hours which was good time for bouncing over the road in Thor the plow truck. I had to work the big hill with about 12-passes to cut the snowpack down to the dirt road for traction. Johnny was able to back down off the big hill and park near the little bridge to sleep while he waited for me to arrive. Johnny thought once he had seen me plow the big hill that I would pull him up the big hill so we could go home. I told johnny that the hill was freshly plowed so it had to set up like concrete when first poured. Johnny said he would sleep more while I went to Kinoosao to plow out the community. That was when I got to see what Thor the plow truck could really do when the tire chains are on the back wheels. When chained up, Thor became a D8 Caterpillar dozer that could push and push snow like you would not believe. I was so impressed at how the USA Air Force had spec'd this truck to be the ultimate snow plowing truck. I was pushing snowbanks back that were 8-feet high, and Thor just pushed and pushed. It only took me an hour to do the snow in Kinoosao including the fish plant which would have taken me 3-hours on a grader. The locals were impressed at how much snow I had moved in such a short time which made their lives easier too. When I returned back to

Johnny sleeping in the semi-truck, I had to wake him up. We hooked the tow strap we use up on the winter roads which are excellent for pulling semi-trucks. I told Johnny I had no idea what Thor was going to pull the big hill like because the scrap guy drove up the big hill the last time Thor was in Kinoosao. I gave Johnny a handheld radio and told him to keep the tow strap tight so there would be no jerking which breaks things. Now I tighten up the tow strap and told Johnny to hang on. I put Thor in 3$^{rd}$ gear on the automatic transmission and held the gas pedal to the floor to let the 250 cummins work as we climbed the hill. Thor pulled the big hill, and I could feel the slight slippage of the expensive tire chains grabbing for tractions. Thor just pulled and pulled and at the top of the big hill, I stopped in the middle of the road. I then walked back to unhook the tow strap. When I walked up to Johnny, he was talking into the handheld radio but there was no sound coming out of my hand-held radio. I pulled out the handheld radio and looked it as Johnny was talking on his. I had bumped the handheld radio to a different channel when I put it in my pocket. When I turned it back to the correct channel, I could then hear Johnny talking which I replied back to him. Jonny then got out of the cab of his semi-truck to explain to me that the speed I was "pulling" his automatic transmission new style semi-truck. The computer had kicked the transmission out of gear thinking it was going to die or something. Thor, the

USA Air Force plow truck had pulled a fully loaded semi-truck up the big hill on the Kinoosao Rally Road as if it was nothing. That explained why it was such a hard pull because I thought Johnny was just keeping the tow strap tight. Now that impressed both of us and Johnny had tried to call on the handheld radio which mine was on the wrong channel. It was our lucky day that we made the big hill, but I also learned a long time ago to cut the snowpack right down.

It was an uneventful trip over the Kinoosao Rally Road as a 2-car parade with Johnny getting back to Grief Rapids at 4am in the morning. The van semi-trailer in Kinoosao was loaded with the totes of fish every 3rd day. Which was cutting it close for fuel for the diesel motor on the refrigeration unit. If the weather did warm up in temperature, it would snow. Then I would have to plow the hills in Thor the plow truck for Johnny to be able to get back from Kinoosao. The fishing was disaster for everyone then it was decided to stop the fishing because everyone went broke. I had to help Johnny with Thor the plow truck on every trip he did to Kinoosao except for the last trip because there was only a ½ of a load in the van semi-trailer. A lot of the fishermen were able to switch from a ski-doo pulling a sleigh to haul the fish to driving new style 4x4 vehicles to get the fish delivered to the fish plant in Kinoosao. A big windstorm came up and drifted in all the packed trails the fishermen had on reindeer lake. A lot of the fishermen had their 4x4 vehicles stuck out on the lake with the fish in the box of the trucks. That was why the last load of fish from Kinoosao was only a partial load with the fish stuck out on the lake.

(hauling the Bombardier to Reindeer Lake)

Now I got asked to help out the fishermen because I owned a bombardier which was built for fishing on frozen lakes. I agreed because I had a little project on reindeer lake, I had been working on for over 20-years. I loaded up the bombardier on my tilt trailer behind the pink crew cab and headed to Kinoosao. The Kinoosao Rally Road was prefect to drive on because I had plowed it correctly with Thor the plow truck. Even when I arrived in Kinoosao, the snow was all plowed correctly like I had done 10-

years ago when I had a "real job" driving a grader. I parked the pink crew cab and unload the bombardier which then required pictures to be taken in front of the Co-op Store. Bob's son joined me for the quick trip out to go Mermaid Hunting.

(the ice roads had a few problems with bad spots)

We had used my side scan sonar to document the semi-truck in storage on the bottom of reindeer lake that fell through the ice. The semi-truck fell through when it found a bad spot in the ice when it was a true ice road to Brochet MB. It was 1998 when the government moved all the ice roads around WHO-ville to travel through the bush to be called winter roads. This semi-truck in storage was a true piece of history to show how dangerous the ice roads can be. I have known about the semi-truck in storage for a long time and even ice fished above it in 2009. When I was engaged to the cop and pussey whipped big time being clean shaven with a 'real job". Then in 2016 instead of spend money foolishly on women. I spent it foolishly on $10,000.00 worth of side scan sonars and under water cameras. Bob's son with Xena and me went out Mermaid Hunting to find the Beech 18 airplane that we recovered, and a few other things include the semi-truck called the Mermaid.

(Bombardier above the Mermaid)

The problem I had was after 20-years of waiting, the pictures of the Mermaid sinking were sent to me in the mail. The pictures of the Mermaid showed a totally different background then when we are at the same location in the summer floating around in a boat. The easiest way to solve the problem was to drive the bombardier out and park on top of the

Mermaid then take a picture which we did. Plus, the trees are not in full bloom so we could figure out the background in the pictures to see if they match. But then again, things change in 40-years since the Mermaid was put into storage. Now that I had the pictures, I needed plus the GPS of the locations. Bob's son, and I could go and tow some vehicles back to Kinoosao. The bombardier was made to the open spaces of reindeer lake. The first vehicle we towed was a dodge that was stuck in deep snow with a load of fish in the back. Then we had to go and find a couple more that needed to be pulled out of the deep snow to the hard packed snow. Then the owners could drive then wherever they wanted to go.

(Bombardier towing a Ford which was fun)

The next one was a Ford, and we could not find it on reindeer lake. Bob's son used my satellite phone to call the owner and they figured it was on the other side of the island that we were at. The Ford was not easy to find because it was white like the snow and reindeer lake had a layer of fog on it being so cold that day. All the other vehicles were easy to find because they were dark in colour. When we arrived at the Ford it was stuck in the snow with a broke transmission from trying to get unstuck. I had to be gentle with the bombardier to jerk the stuck Ford out, but I did it. Bob's son was able to get the Ford running in the cold temperature which surprised me.

(the fog off in the distance on Reindeer Lake)

Now we only had 20-miles to travel back to Kinoosao which would not take long. The Ford was putting out enough heat to keep Bob's son warm while I was too warm in the bombardier. The motor was in the back of the bombardier which heats up the inside very well plus I had 2-brand new heaters installed to make it really warm.

On the last narrow stretch to Kinoosao, we passed a vehicle that drove down the ice from Brochet MB. The snow was giving the vehicle a hard time, so it was slow moving. The people were looking at the bombardier going speeding passed because there had not been a bombardier on reindeer lake in 30-years. When we arrived in Kinoosao, I was able to get the broken Ford off the ice and up in the community. Then I had to go back out of the frozen lake and pull the vehicle we had passed off the lake. The snow was just too deep and hard for the vehicle which only hard 2-wheel drive because 4x4 had broken early in their trip. The bombardier did well, and we had fun on reindeer lake with lots of good pictures and film taken. I took fish out of the back of the vehicles we towed as payment. I knew the fishermen did not make any money trying to winter fish. The drive back to the Kingdom was excellent and when I arrived, I shared the pictures of the fun on reindeer lake with my Kingdom Followers around the world.

This is end of the 8th book in the 8-book series on Winter Roads ending in the year 2019. My book series will continue in the future as we have more fun and adventures on the winter roads in Northern Manitoba Canada.    June 2021 thansk

(looking good at -40F in the heat of the day)

# ABOUT THE AUTHOR

Joey Barnes, who is also known as the King of Obsolete, grew up in a small town called Alexander, Manitoba in a pink house which is grey to him being colour blind.

In the mid 1990's he moved to the town of Lynn Lake, Manitoba and he lives on the outskirts of town with his daughter Xena. He commonly refers to his home as the Kingdom. (What else would a "King" call his home?)

Joey Barnes became involved in the scrap metal recycling industry in the early 1980's recycling scrap throughout northern Manitoba. The high costs of transportation and residential criticism made this a constant battle so in 2004/2005 he was obliged to remove most of his scrap metal recyclables.

The Kingdom contains many recycled and historical items. The King of Obsolete still uses the 1939 Chevrolet that he bought for $200.00 in 1984. Most of the King of Obsoletes equipment is from the 1940's and 1950's and is used regularly. The King's Cats have been recycled or brought back to life by remodeling them and using whatever parts are available to create the winter freighting cats. These are used by the King of Obsolete for winter freighting and building winter roads.

The King of Obsolete enjoys his life in the Kingdom where it is a little different. There are no restaurants in the town, no shopping malls, no fast-food delivery or banks. Most supplies are bought in from Thompson, Manitoba and hauled over the 300 km "so called road". Some goods are shipped from southern communities.

Being a single parent of a daughter, a published author then on national TV around the world with 15 seconds of fame. This makes the King of Obsolete known in faraway places. The computers make the world a small place to keep in touch with his Kingdom Followers.

Now with the Covid 19 lock downs in the year 2020 which has made the world come to a halt. The King of Obsolete used this time to write new books based on his wasted youth growing up in the south which was a different time and place compared to today's world we live in. To see more of the King's lifestyle please check him out online at: www.kingofobsolete.ca

Thansk